THE UNIQUE INDIVIDUAL *You*

NAOMI HARM

YOUR COMPASS, VISIONARY ROADMAP, AND TOOLKIT
TO BECOME A TRANSFORMATIONAL LEADER

Printed in the United States of America

Published in Hellertown, PA

Cover design by Kristen Williams

Cover photo edited by Serferis

Library of Congress Control Number: 2021912069

ISBN 978-1-952481-61-1

2 4 6 8 10 9 7 5 3 1

For more information or to place bulk orders,

contact the publisher at Jennifer@BrightCommunications.net.

Bright
COMMUNICATIONS

TO EVERY WOMAN LEADER AND ENTREPRENEUR PURSUING YOUR DREAM CAREER

May this book serve as a compass for your leadership journey and a visionary roadmap to help you identify your true inner leadership calling. This is just the beginning, as you discover your influence of the unique individual you. Remember to invest in yourself and your personal well-being, to lead with purpose, and to prioritize your happiness as you embark on your new leadership adventure.

CONTENTS

Women Leaders 6

Do you want to build your leadership confidence, cognitive presence, and sphere of influence? 6

Chapter 1: My Leadership Story 9

The Gift of Neuroscience 9

My Family's Story 11

Putting Purpose into Practice 23

Chapter 2: Our Big Beautiful Brains Are Wired for Leadership 25

Women Think Differently Than Men 25

The Impact of COVID-19 on Women's Careers 28

Putting Purpose into Practice 31

Chapter 3: Your Leadership Purpose and Inner Calling 35

Identify Your Leadership Purpose and Your Inner Calling 35

Inner Work versus Outer Work 40

Putting Purpose into Practice 48

Chapter 4: Make the Leadership Experience Transformational 52

Childhood and Lifetime Experiences Define Your Leadership Style 52

Leadership Habits and Routines 61

Modeling Empathy, Intuition, and Collaboration 67

Putting Purpose into Practice 75

Chapter 5: Grow Your Leadership Confidence 76

Connecting the Learning Dots with an Educational Leadership Influence 76

Creating a Culture of Feedback for Successful Communication and Collaboration 81

Putting Purpose into Practice 91

Chapter 6: The Art of Active Listening to Understand and Empathize with Others 93

Building an Empathetic Workforce 93

Understanding Body Language 104

Putting Purpose into Practice 109

Chapter 7: The Pursuit of Happiness 112

Enjoy Professional Achievement and Personal Fulfillment Without Feeling Guilty. *112*

Finding Balance to Honor Professional and Personal Learning *112*

Investing in Yourself: Healthy Boundaries and Self-Compassion *117*

Putting Purpose into Practice *121*

Chapter 8: Lean-in Leadership Engagement Strategies 127

Knowing When to Lean In to Support Courageous Conversations *127*

Learning Phrases to Engage in Positive Conversations *130*

Improving Your Active Listening and Self-Awareness Leadership Skills. *133*

Putting Purpose into Practice *137*

Chapter 9: Leadership Connections + Lasting Relationships 140

Building Leadership Connections and Lasting Relationships. . . . *140*

Understanding the Power of Names. *146*

Putting Purpose into Practice *148*

Chapter 10: Celebrate the Unique Individual You 151

Creating Your Legacy, Story, and Positive Influence. *151*

Deciding How to Mentor Young Women Leaders. *155*

Putting Purpose into Practice *160*

In Closing: 164

Resources: 165

Acknowledgements: 174

About the Author: 177

Prologue

WOMEN LEADERS

Do you want to build your leadership confidence, cognitive presence, and sphere of influence?

In *The Unique Individual You,* I present compelling neuroscience research that documents how and why women's brains are wired for empathy, intuition, and collaboration—the very qualities business managers and educational administrators are looking for in their leaders of today. Mentorship stories of hope, optimism, mindfulness, and resilience drive the storyline, and they outline a creative visionary roadmap of effective "lean-in" strategies and solutions from women leaders that you can use to define and guide your own career trajectory.

Over more than 25 years, I have developed established and effective facilitation methods that model outstanding women in leadership strategies, mentoring techniques, and Total Participation Techniques (TPT) methods. These compassion-based conversations, professional development sessions, and keynotes have transformed businesses and the educational relationships of community practices worldwide.

If your actions create a legacy that inspires others to dream more, learn more, do more, and become more, then you are an excellent leader.
—Dolly Parton

In this book, you'll learn about my personal struggles as a woman leader in the IT and STEM industry. I'll highlight how I overcame setbacks and recognized my success in inspiring others with the knowledge I've gained in the K-12 educational field, the corporate world of big business, and through personal and technical lessons I've learned as CEO of my EdTech women-in-leadership organization.

You'll discover women-in-leadership practices that explain how and why you should develop and invest in an organization's talent: its employees. These strategies provide you with leadership tools to reach your professional and personal goals, while making a significant impact on the organization you work for and represent.

In addition, each chapter includes an action-oriented tool kit, such as the following:

- Empathy-based coaching
- Relationship building with gender techniques
- Mentoring and relationship culture-building activities
- Reading-the-room methods on when to lean in and when to observe consciously
- Body language and conversational tone techniques to represent your best self and model your sphere of influence
- Tips to be more present in your everyday leadership experiences and conversations
- Strategies for investing in yourself with thoughtful, social emotional learning (SEL) and self-care habits
- The importance of beginning and finishing each day with a moment of gratitude
- Impactful strategies to leave your legacy of good by mentoring our aspiring future women leaders

I'll also present a plethora of snapshot learning scenarios and call-for-action reflection pieces on how to lead with integrity when inspiring others with your creative and positive genius, so that you, too, can influence and build your leadership confidence. (You'll see that I often use the word "learning" throughout this book, such as describing scenarios as "learning scenarios." This is because as an educator, I view life through the lens of education.) In addition, I have provided supportive leadership models, tools, resources, and educational protocols to guide you with leadership expertise as you begin developing your leadership visionary roadmap. Perhaps most profoundly, you will discover your inner calling to honor, invest in, and mentor our future generations of young women leaders with engaging and influential learner centered approaches.

Good leaders organize and align people around what the team needs to do. Great leaders motivate and inspire people with why they're doing it. That's purpose. And that's the key to achieving something truly transformational.

—Marillyn Hewson

Visit the site to access this book's support toolkit of resources and the reflection workbook to support your learning from each chapter.

Chapter 1

MY LEADERSHIP STORY

Gratitude Is the Best Attitude

THE GIFT OF NEUROSCIENCE

My love for neuroscience and educational studies began during my undergraduate years studying to become a K-12 teacher in the early 1990s. The educational and foundational courses required by my alma mater, Viterbo University, were a secret passage to knowledge and a hidden gift of new learning experience that really intrigued me as a graduate. It opened the door to learning opportunities and new learning passions on the purpose and value of action-based study.

As a teacher and mother of three elementary-school-age boys at the time, I tried to better understand and apply the four stages of cognitive development and brain research that were developed by Jean Piaget, PhD, a Swiss child development psychologist. I tried to perfect my understanding of my own children and the students in my classroom, and to be better able to respond to them with compassion and empathy.

I was intrigued to apply these brain-based neuroscience coping strategies to comfort and guide my children and students as they responded to circumstances and stressors in their lives. Such circumstances and stressors included trauma from family activities, joy from learning moments, disappointments from losing a sport or other recreational game, and satisfaction from completing a mission or challenging assignment with dedication. As I applied the best-studied teaching and learning methods to solve issues and formulate theories, I felt like I was teleported to a new job of being a neuroscience analyst and mathematician.

All in all, my children and students turned out to be perfectly fine. The benefit is that they were nurtured by a very caring, empathetic mother and educator. I always enjoyed leading my children and my students on their learning journeys. I loved empowering them to make their own choices that led to good decisions (most of the time) and to follow through on their behaviors to ensure a positive learning effect.

Looking back, I think that many educators are unaware of the relevance and validity of brain-based learning science in education. It is a real differentiator and contributor, making the difference between a good teacher and an outstanding teacher. Knowledge is strength. When we take new learning seriously and adapt it effectively to our everyday personal and professional lives, it can change learning outcomes tremendously. In particular, it promotes our vital positions in the classroom as influential, caring educators. It can also enhance our value in our relationships with colleagues and even family members.

I've always been intrigued by how our big beautiful brains function. I'm fascinated by how our neural sensors capture, view, evaluate, and process the immense amount of knowledge that we need to filter through each day. I'm amazed how our brains begin to develop, bind, and reconnect with activated neurons to create new learning pathways and to reinforce the neuroplasticity of the brain that is forever malleable, to enhance our creative thinking and intellect.

Neuroscience is by far the most exciting branch of science because the brain is the most fascinating object in the universe. Every human brain is different. The brain makes each human unique and defines who he or she is.
—Stanley B. Prusiner

MY FAMILY'S STORY

Neuroscience has been so relevant in my life. It's been even more so since my youngest son, Jacob, incurred a major traumatic brain injury (TBI) in a line-of-duty accident while he was serving in the US Army in April 2014. He was just 19 years old.

After a serious motor vehicle accident that severely broke Jacob's physical body, he was in a coma for more than two weeks with no evidence of recovery. The accident had fractured many bones in Jacob's body, from his shoulder blades to his lower back to his pelvis. It had broken both of his femurs, his knees, tibias, his left ankle, and multiple bones in his feet to the tips of his toes. It had also left him with paralysis on the left side of his body, due to an injury on the right side of his brain. This condition is known as hemiplegia.

Hemiplegia occurs because each side of the brain controls movement on the opposite side of the body. Certain parts of the brain send a complex array of signals to the muscles in the body, enabling you to move them on command. When a TBI damages these areas of the brain, those signals can become interrupted. As a result, the muscles are not able to respond to the brain's directions, and paralysis can set in.

We were devastated. There was nothing we could do. We could only wait to see how much Jacob could recover.

In the first two weeks after Jacob's accident, he received multiple MRI and CAT scans. The neurosurgeons and trauma doctors spoke to Jacob's dad and me regularly to provide us with information on Jacob's brain function and whether or not any improvement had been achieved. Jacob did have brain activity, which gave us hope. Beyond that, Jacob's doctors did not give us a bright prognosis. They told us that Jacob would likely be in a vegetative condition for a very long time, and he most likely would require 100 percent care for the rest of his life. They recommended he be sent to a long-term nursing home once released from the trauma hospital.

We were distraught when we heard "vegetative condition" and "long-term nursing home." We clung to the hope of a better outcome for Jacob, encouraged by tiny signs of improvement. Jacob squeezed our hands intermittently when we spoke to him softly. He often had a twitch under his eyelids, and we could see that his eyes were flickering very slightly. We knew Jacob was in there. We knew he could hear us, but he didn't wake up yet.

For three weeks after Jacob's accident, he was kept in a sedated coma. He also must have been very tired as he struggled to heal from his injuries.

We trusted Jacob, and we believed in his ability to heal. Jacob had youth on his side. He was also in excellent physical shape from his Army training and workouts. We were told that this probably saved his life. But it was Jacob's intellect—his big beautiful brain—that we wanted to better understand. I knew that he would need to relearn how to do even the most basic tasks. He would also need to learn new skills to navigate his future world. I knew his life would never be the same.

Days and weeks passed. We didn't see any change or improvement. Jacob still laid lifeless in his hospital bed. I felt fear, hopelessness, and a complete loss of understanding. We were advised to be patient.

"All of this will take time, and every brain injury and outcome is different for each person," the doctors said.

Jacob's brain needed to heal and recover.

The doctors had postponed the surgeries that Jacob needed to repair all his fractured bones. Surgery would be too traumatic and dangerous for Jacob in his comatose state. His dad and I agreed.

To make matters worse, my husband, Jeff, and I observed that Jacob was being treated as a number—not a person—in this facility. After 40 long days of that, Jeff and I knew we needed to move Jacob out of this hell of a dilapidated facility. We searched for options to airlift Jacob out of Texas and back to our home state of Minnesota, where the healthcare services were exceptional.

During this time in Texas, Jeff and I had some very difficult talks. We had to make many hard decisions about what to do as a family to take care of Jacob. We did not want Jacob to be treated in the VA system, which at that time had a poor reputation of care for its own injured warrior veterans.

Jeff and I debated which of us should give up his or her career to be Jacob's full-time caregiver. The other one of us needed to continue working to provide for our family unit of three. We would need to survive on only one income.

We decided that I would keep running my business as CEO, and my husband would leave his position as an IT network administrator of our Innovative Educator Consulting company. We both struggled with this decision. The implications were significant. All the pressure would now be on me to provide our family with financial stability. At the same time, my husband would give up his career in IT, and his workplace social life.

Within just five days after Jacob's military accident, I had to leave the hospital in Texas and travel to Canada to deliver a keynote address and a series of seminars for 300 K-12 educators. I didn't have the option to say no because it was a paying consultancy job. We needed the money to help our family move forward financially and create a new normal.

I was agonized leaving my son, who was still in a coma. I also felt guilty leaving Jeff alone to advocate for Jacob. At that point, I knew more than ever that we had to get Jacob back to Minnesota!

I had a very successful presentation event in Canada with the Saskatoon Library Media Association. I also had several very candid late-night conversations with some of the most creative, intelligent women educational leaders in Canada. For the first time in a long time, I felt empowered. These women encouraged me to continue onward—to be strong, to be brave, and to be bold.

They also reminded me to lead with compassion, gratitude, and purpose. They shared from their own experiences that the trials and tribulations I was currently going through would eventually pass. They helped me to see that these experiences would contribute to my next chapter and story. I understood that I would be able to share these life lessons and eventually leave my women-in-leadership legacy for others to learn from.

I was so grateful. Coincidentally, the women gifted me a gratitude book, *What Makes You Grateful?* by Anne O. Kubitsky. The gift was so fitting to complement the story I had confided in them about my son and why he means the world to me.

That's when I knew karma was on my side, and *she* was watching over me with the guidance from this women-in-leadership group. These women became my North Star, helping me see the light in all of the darkness of the trauma that I was experiencing. These women leaders, and other women leaders I have met since, guide me in my learning discoveries, my women-in-leadership career, and my entrepreneurial business.

The words of wisdom and honest reflections from these creative, intelligent women gave me the right balance of emotional support, optimism, and hope to create my visionary roadmap, my pathway to extensive educational research.

From the support of these Canadian women educational leaders, whom I now call my very good friends, I knew I needed to reflect on this learning journey. I knew it was the only way for me to stay strong, both personally and professionally.

My talks with these women inspired me to create an accountability log to share with Jacob later in his life. I wanted to provide him with true daily accounts and an accurate story of what happened to him. Logging and journaling kept me focused on neuroscience research, which gave me—and eventually Jacob—a lens on learning to help us pursue alternative healthcare solutions for my son. At that time, Jacob could not make those decisions for himself.

To read the original blog that captured Jacob's entire seven-year journey from his accident to the present, go to *https://posthope.org/we-love-jake.* It encapsulates the entire family's transformation, which helped all of us appreciate the value and importance of neuroscience. It also helped us to realize how special one's big beautiful brain is. It has the power to rebuild itself from a traumatic injury because its plasticity allows its malleability.

Jacob's journey reinforced for me that one must never, ever give up hope. With optimism and gratitude, and by leading with compassion, insight, and strength, a family can recover from a traumatic event.

It seemed like Jacob was in a coma for an eternity. Yet this long wait was what Jacob needed to heal his broken body and brain before he could wake to face his new reality. At that time, we knew that Jacob would live with a cognitive impairment for the rest of his life. We still didn't know if Jacob would ever talk or walk again.

The waiting time gave my husband and me the opportunity to do extensive research to get up to speed on neuroscience and to find the best Minnesota traumatic brain injury and recovery facility—Bethesda Hospital, in Saint Paul, Minnesota. This facility is one of the top five in the nation. We wanted to provide Jacob with the medical care he so needed and deserved.

Yet I wondered how we, as parents, could convince the commanding officer of Fort Bliss in Texas to authorize Jacob's transfer to a specialized traumatic brain injury facility thousands of miles away.

First, my husband and I had several painful conversations with the US Army medical team in charge of our son's care, which was not providing us much guidance or compassion. Then we had two face-to-face conversations with the commanding officer of Fort Bliss. We advocated and fought like hell to convince the commander to allow us to move Jacob to get the necessary TBI care that our son was not receiving in Texas. The commander heard our pleas, acknowledged that the US Army medical team was not providing the level of care Jacob needed due to the severity of his accident and TBI, and acknowledged that we as a family had a choice in Jacob's medical care.

We are very thankful that US Army Colonel Mike Heimall, under the direction of the Fort Bliss Army commander, took the next steps to pursue and apply a signed waiver to allow for our son to be airlifted from Texas to Bethesda Hospital's TBI Center in Minnesota. This would override the denial of transportation by TriCare United Healthcare, which occurred. If the waiver was accepted it would allow for Jacob to be airlifted back to Minnesota for the needed and deserved TBI and wound care from his military accident. Yet we still had to wait. Jacob could not be released until he had fully awoken from his coma and could be stabilized for a two-hour flight back to Minnesota. By day 28, Jacob was more stable and alert, and the induced coma was almost fully worn off. He was beginning to wake up. He was still very weak. We had to be so careful not to overstimulate him, which could cause a setback or even death.

Jacob did not know where he was nor what had happened. He could not speak. He squeezed our hands to respond to very short questions with "yes" or "no" answers. It was apparent he knew who Jeff and I were, yet he didn't recognize anyone else. We knew Jacob was in there, but we wouldn't know how much of our Jacob was truly there until much later in his recovery.

By day 40, we were given the go-ahead to prepare for Jacob's flight within the next seven days if he remained stable. To prepare, Jeff stayed with Jacob in the trauma center in Texas, and I flew to Minnesota to be on the receiving end at Bethesda Hospital and fill out the paperwork, talk with the medical team, and be there when Jacob arrived. Jeff and I wanted to ensure Jacob was never left alone. We wanted him to know that he had a parent advocating for him as he prepared to leave Texas, and that he had another parent ready to advocate for him upon his arrival at the new hospital.

In my research, I learned that having a consistent routine is important for recovery and healing for people with TBI. They need to feel they have a sense of control over their changed world. I was proactive in following this advice from day one to model and build upon these skills to support our son's new learning routines.

Finally, by day 43, Jacob was stable enough to move and endure the two-hour flight. He was airlifted out of Texas—along with a full staff of medics and registered nurses on a US military jet. They transferred him to Bethesda Hospital in Saint Paul, Minnesota, where he stayed for the next 80 days.

It was at Bethesda Hospital that Jacob learned how to chew and swallow again. It's also where he learned to speak again. I will never forget his first post-accident sentence, delivered as best he could in a flat, monotone voice 90 days after his accident.

"I love you, Mom."

Jacob had to read this simple sentence from a sheet of paper. His kind, patient speech therapist, April, had lettered it for him in block print.

When Jacob uttered his first post-accident words, I sobbed uncontrollably for the next half hour, clutching Jacob and April.

That day, I realized—I really knew and understood—that my Jacob was still in that broken body. We just needed to awaken his learning senses with techniques validated by neuroscience and brain-based learning activities.

To me, this experience with Jacob confirmed how very precious our brains are. I began to understand how brain neurons connect to learning experiences through active sensory motor movements. I learned why it's so important to continue making mental and visual associations for long-term and short-term memory loss after an injury.

I was so deeply grateful to those caring healthcare professionals, who collaborated so closely and compassionately with Jacob to direct his new understanding. They retrained his brain to be able to read and speak again. I need to thank one compassionate RN, Amy Dulmage, as she endured the entire journey with us while Jacob was at Bethesda. She was truly Jacob's guardian angel. In the brief moments of time when Jeff and I were not there, she ensured Jacob was well taken care of. She was always there to assist us and remind us to catch up on a few hours of sleep or to take a quick shower so we could stay strong for Jacob.

My sister Renee Matt, her husband, Rick, and Jacob's cousins Damien, Jesse, and Sage from Iowa were also sources of support and influence during these trying times. They wanted to do something, to help us, as they are also Jacob's godparents. Due to the healing process waiting game for Jacob, there was not much they could do. Yet Renee sent several caregiver gift packages to the hospital focused on health and wellness for Jeff and me. Perhaps the most special gift that was sent to us was the hand designed "Fight, Fight, Fight and Never Give Up" banner that we proudly displayed in Jacob's Bethesda hospital room and subsequent healthcare facilities until we could bring Jacob home.

It provided us hope, strength, and optimism from my beloved sister, Renee. In return, it felt like the entire family was there to help, guide, and support us every day. The banner was a visual guide of my sister's compassionate leadership, reminding us to stay positive, and reassuring us that we were truly surrounded by our loved ones, even though they were far away. I also practiced this inner strength modeled by my sister when faced with future adversity and difficult situations.

As Jacob made progress over the next few months, my heart filled with more hope. I vowed to share my family's experience to help others use lessons from neuroscience in every kind of work we do.

Neuroscience provides a guide to recognize ourselves and realize our future perspectives on life. It outlines human-centered experiences and explains how we understand people, places, and events in our lives. It prepares us to connect and interact efficiently with others. It helps us to know how to respond with empathetic listening ears, hearts, and minds when we are faced with the critical situations that we experience daily.

As I read more about neuroscience research, I had an epiphany: I finally understood why my women–leadership focus is so important to me and why I continue to lead and operate my leadership business. My experience with Jacob's accident and recovery and my research on traumatic brain injury drove me to lead with empathy, intuition, and collaboration. This turned my little-known company into a globally renowned, influential educational organization.

Three months after his accident, Jacob had recovered enough to move on to the next steps in his recovery process. Jacob needed to become healthy enough that his body could mend his fractured femurs, pelvis, knees, and feet. He needed to rebuild his stamina to begin physical therapy, and he needed to regain his balance to finally walk again. It was a long, daunting road.

Jacob's doctors stressed that it was important for him to regain his balance as soon as possible. This surprised me, but I learned equilibrium needs to be regained in a very timely manner following a TBI because it has a beneficial effect on the regeneration of the brain's plasticity. Equilibrium activates the brain's ability to bind, grow, and alter neuronal connections.

Every time we make new connections and develop new skills—for example if we learn new emotional intelligence tactics—we learn to improve these neuronal connections to develop new attitudes and habits. Using learning opportunities like this, Jacob started his cognitive and physical learning journey.

It was fascinating to see how much of Jacob's physical recovery was dependent upon and driven by his brain's recovery. Jeff and I knew it was important that Jacob understood his current learning options. We showed Jacob pictures of people, places, and events, and we retold family stories to help him recall and rebuild the memories that he had lost due to his injury. We helped

THE RANCHO LOS AMIGOS LEVELS OF COGNITIVE FUNCTIONING

Level 1* • *No Response: Person appears to be in a deep sleep.

Level 2* • *Generalized Response: Person reacts inconsistently and not directly in response to stimuli.

Level 3* • *Localized Response: Person reacts inconsistently and directly to stimuli.

Level 4* • *Confused/Agitated: Person is extremely agitated and confused.

Level 5* • *Confused-Inappropriate/Non-agitated: Person is confused, and responses to commands are inaccurate.

Level 6* • *Confused-Appropriate: Person is confused and responds accurately to commands.

Level 7* • *Automatic-Appropriate: Person can go through daily routine with minimal to no confusion.

Level 8* • *Purposeful-Appropriate: Person has functioning memory and is aware of and responsive to their environment.

Level 9* • *Purposeful-Appropriate: Person can go through daily routine while aware of need for stand-by assistance.

Level 10* • *Purposeful-Appropriate/Modified Independent: Person can go through daily routine but may require more time or compensatory strategies.

Jacob reconstruct his past so that he could have a feeling of influence over his new life.

As Jacob's parents and advocates, we needed to make sure that he had access to tools and resources to promote his new way of learning. We refused to accept the ill-fated prognosis that we were offered in Texas. Instead, we dove into neuroscience. We focused on all the new brain research. We read all of the most up-to-date neuroscience studies we could find. We let the science lead every decision we made, in collaboration with Bethesda Hospital's doctors and nurses.

The compassionate care Jacob received at Bethesda Hospital forever altered our vision of our lives and our son's life. The staff gave us confidence and inspiration as they actively listened to our questions and directed us to better empower ourselves as parents and full-time caregivers.

One tool they gave us is the Rancho Skills Matrix brain injury neuroscience study. This matrix helped steer our perceptions—and eliminate our misconceptions—of Jacob's disabilities and his future. This tool helped us to understand the critical treatment he'd require for a lifetime and the stages in healing he would go through. We were told that some patients only heal to a certain Rancho Skills Matrix level and never recover beyond that, so we had to be prepared and fully aware of what to expect now as lifetime caregivers to Jacob.

When Jacob left Bethesda Hospital, he moved one step closer to home—the Red Wing, Minnesota, Physical Therapy Recovery Center. Jeff and I lived there with Jacob for 40 days, building up his courage and strength, regaining his balance, and introducing the use of a wheelchair. At that time, Jacob usually had to hold onto supporting balancing beams to stand.

During our 40 days at Red Wing, Jeff and I gained more nursing experience. For example, we learned how to make the bed-to-wheelchair transition, helping Jacob move from his bed to his wheelchair safely and comfortably. At that time, we didn't know if Jacob would ever walk again, so he needed to learn how to navigate life in a wheelchair.

As our 40 days at Red Wing wound down, we could see the homestretch. We moved Jacob from Red Wing to Gundersen Healthcare in La-crosse, Wisconsin, which was only 10 miles away from our then-home in Brownsville, Minnesota.

RECOVERY TWO YEARS AFTER BRAIN INJURY

Based on information of people with moderate to severe TBI who received acute medical care and inpatient rehabilitation services at a TBI Model System, two years post-injury:

Most people continue to show decreases in disability.

- 34 percent require some level of supervision during the day and/or night.
- 93 percent are living in a private residence.
- 34 percent are living with their spouse or significant other; 29 percent are living with their parents.
- 33 percent are employed; 29 percent are unemployed; 26 percent are retired due to any reason; and 3 percent are students.

Jacob stayed at Gundersen Healthcare for two weeks. He started to develop confidence in walking with the assistance of a walker—and the help of a nurse, Jeff, or me. During Jacob's two weeks at Gundersen, he regained enough strength to finally come home.

Over the next two years at home, Jacob had daily outpatient physical therapy care at Gundersen. He also needed several more operations on his legs and feet to help him regain the ability to walk independently. Jacob took his first new steps 18 months after his accident. Today, Jacob walks completely unaided—though with his own unique style of walking.

At home, Jacob continued to have speech therapy to restore his speech and voice quality. Therapy also helped Jacob regain some inflection in his voice.

Although we brought Jacob back to a quality-functioning stage, he will have a lifelong cognitive learning disability of delayed thinking, decision-making, and communicating. Jacob also has large motor physical disabilities, with left side partial paralysis. He currently comprehends at a middle-school level. He falls on the Rancho Los Amigos Levels of Cognitive Functioning scale between levels 6 and 7.

Jacob's accident and severe TBI also transformed his personality. It impacted his everyday ability to communicate and interact with other people for life. With all that said, today Jacob enjoys a quality lifestyle that can adapt to his varying capacity requirements. That's all that counts.

Jacob taught me—a mother and educator—some of the most valuable lessons in life. He encouraged me to be an active participant in his recovery and learning. Being a responsible, patient, and supportive parent to an adult child with a serious disability has been the biggest challenge of my life by far. Yet it made me 10 times stronger!

In addition to making me a more compassionate mother, these experiences also helped me in my professional life. I discovered how to better plan, organize, connect, and run my global women-in-leadership business—and at the same time provide for my family.

When life hands you a horrific challenge, family is the most important element to heal, nurture, love, aid, and pave the road to a successful recovery. Every TBI story is different. The healing timeframes vary greatly among individuals. People who are willing to accept the challenge, forgive the past, and lead with a positive growth mindset (to discover the future of the "what-if's" and endless learning potentials of what is yet to come) are well on the way to finding happiness!

Putting Purpose into Practice

FIND GRATITUDE

The word "gratitude" is derived from the Latin word gratiaital, which means kindness, graciousness, or gratitude, depending on the context. Gratitude is a feeling of love for what one has been given. The gift can be physical or intangible.

Gratitude offers many benefits to our lives. People who are grateful understand the quality of goodness in their lives. Generally, people understand that this goodness originates from beyond themselves. Gratitude keeps things in perspective, and it helps people realize that they are important to the bigger picture.

Psychology studies find gratitude to be greatly, reliably correlated with greater satisfaction in life. Gratitude uplifts the spirit, brings out feelings of joy, aids people in difficult times, and strengthens people's ability to cope with stress and difficult relationships.

People express gratitude and appreciation in different ways. Some do so by reliving past experiences, recalling happy times, and expressing thanks for aspects of their childhood or past blessings. Others might focus on the present by not taking good fortune for granted when it comes. Still, others might look to the future with a hopeful, optimistic attitude. Regardless of your intrinsic or actual degree of appreciation, it is an attitude that can be effectively cultivated further.

Gratitude teaches people to accept what they have, rather than constantly looking for something different, expecting that the thing they pursue will make them happy, or believing that they can't be fulfilled until all of their needs are met. Gratitude allows people to focus on what they have rather than what they lack. Although it can seem contrived at first, this emotional state strengthens with use and practice.

Next are a few suggestions for cultivating gratitude. I encourage and challenge you to try one act of gratitude per day for 30 days to create a positive habit, which will also fill your happiness bucket.

WRITE A THANK YOU NOTE

Writing a thank you note to someone expressing your appreciation of that person's effect on your life might make you happier and strengthen your relationship with that person. Send the note, or if possible, deliver it and read it in person. Set a goal of sending at least one appreciation letter every month. Write one to yourself every now and then too. You could write it on a Post-it Note and place it where you can see it to bring a smile to your face.

MENTALLY THANK OTHERS

Don't have time to write a thank you note? It can help to remember someone who has done something good for you and mentally thank them.

KEEP A GRATITUDE JOURNAL

Make it a habit to write about the gifts you've received each day. I start and end each day with a moment of gratitude, to affirm my completed tasks, celebrate new learning, and note my leadership connection gains.

LIST YOUR BLESSINGS

Set aside some time each week to write about your blessings, focusing on what went well or what you are thankful for. It helps to choose a number of items to list each week, such as three to five. Be descriptive in your writing and also consider writing about the feelings you had when something positive happened to you.

PRAY

If you are spiritual, you can foster gratitude through prayer because it provides moments of quiet, self-reflection, and calm in your day.

MEDITATE

The practice of mindful meditation involves concentrating on the present moment without judgment. Some people meditate by concentrating on a single word or expression, such as "peace." You can also concentrate on what you are grateful for, such as the warmth of the sun or a pleasant sound.

ARE YOU LOOKING FOR MORE WAYS TO EXPRESS YOUR GRATITUDE?

Here is a collection of 10-Minute Gratitude Journals to assist your efforts. Feel free to download, print, and share with others to spread the gift of gratitude.

Chapter 2

OUR BIG BEAUTIFUL BRAINS ARE WIRED FOR LEADERSHIP

Successful Women Think Differently

WOMEN THINK DIFFERENTLY THAN MEN

To better understand the role of neuroscience and brain development in our lives, we need to understand how women's and men's minds differ. Then we need to discover how this influences the way we operate businesses and organizations.

In his 1992 book *Men Are from Mars, Women Are from Venus,* John Gray, PhD, focused on variations in communication patterns between men and women. For example, men often seek to fix issues, while women usually want to discuss them.

Recent evidence indicates this may potentially be the product of variations between women's and men's brains. A research study in the August 2017 issue of the *Journal of Alzheimer's Disease* revealed that women's brains are slightly more involved in some ways and more active in certain areas than men's brains.

In his book *Unleash the Power of the Female Brain,* Daniel G. Amen, MD, noted that women's brains are wired for success. The "CEO section of the brain"—the prefrontal cortex that governs perception, organization, impulse control, and planning—is more powerful in women. This means that women are wired to assume positions of authority. Dr. Amen and his colleagues completed the largest brain-image analysis ever performed. Their thesis included the comparison of single-photon emission computerized tomography (SPECT) scans of 26,000 participants. Their most important discovery was that women had slightly more blood flow in the brain in 112 of the 128 regions they measured.

"I thought there would be differences, but I had no idea they'd be this significant," Dr. Amen wrote.

In addition to enhanced activity in the prefrontal cortex, the brains of women also showed more blood flow in the limbic or emotional areas, which involve mood, anxiety, and depression. The hippocampus, or the memory center, was also more active in women's brains.

"If I make my wife mad, she doesn't forget it," Dr. Amen half-joked in his book.

Dr. Amen's study found that men's brains, on the other hand, had more blood flow in the visual and coordination centers. Dr. Amen suggested that the research confirms the hypothesis that men have very fine "tunnel vision," while women may have better "peripheral vision."

"The results also indicate that the female brain is wired for leadership," Dr. Amen wrote.

Another area of the brain that has elevated activation in women is called the insular cortex, which is an area of the brain associated with empathy and intuition. This could explain why many women spend more time than most men worrying about what other people are thinking. But this also might explain why women communicate well with others, because it takes a lot of brain activity in the insular cortex to read and engage with others, Dr. Amen wrote.

Due to this heightened brain function, women appear to have stronger abilities than men in the fields of:

- **Empathy:** the desire to share or appreciate the thoughts of another person
- **Intuition:** knowing that something is real without knowing precisely why
- **Collaboration:** the desire to work together with other people for a shared purpose (This is another key reason why women often make such great bosses.)
- **Self-control:** the ability to control one's emotions or desires (This points to women's decreased incidence of speeding, drug abuse, and even their chances of going to prison.)
- **Necessary worry:** the type of caring for others that helps to keep them safe (Women tend to worry about and take care of their well-being and that of their families more effectively than men do. This argument is fascinating. A major survey found that "don't worry, be happy" people, most often men on motorcycles, died earlier from crashes and preventable disease. Necessary worry may be one reason why women live longer than men.)

Females are neurologically well-suited to guide people, handle situations, and solve the world's biggest problems. Yet, since the beginning of the human race, men have been in positions of authority. Although society's advancement is remarkable, we still face conflict, challenges, power struggles, ill health, and more every day. Through recognizing and respecting the potential of women's brains, we will inspire girls and women to use their brains to change the world.

A fascinating article published in the June 2011 *Harvard Business Review* titled "What Makes a Team Smarter? More Women" addressed a study in which teams were assigned a variety of tasks, including brainstorming, decision-making, and problem-solving. The teams received cumulative intelligence scores based on their results, called group IQ.

Can you guess which teams did better? If you guessed that it was the teams that had higher individual IQ scores, you would be wrong. The teams that had a higher group IQ were the teams with more women.

Understanding both the gifts and the challenges of how women's big beautiful brains work will help women take advantage of the strength of the female brain to achieve the success they deserve. Now, more than ever, we need "brain-smart," insightful, knowledgeable, creative, influential women to lead and redirect our neighborhoods, our churches, our jobs, our country, and our planet.

THE IMPACT OF COVID-19 ON WOMEN'S CAREERS

Before the COVID-19 pandemic, women were still grappling for gender representation in workplaces around the world. There were few ways to advance our skills as women entrepreneurs, CEOs, and senior managers in today's major EdTech corporate environments, industry organizations, and K-12 education systems.

Then the pandemic hit. And things certainly didn't get better.

The COVID-19 pandemic had a devastating impact on our country, and it has taken a huge toll on women in particular. Research suggests that it will set women back by at least half a decade, if not more, as many women had to choose between their careers and taking care of their families.

According to the 2020 *Women in the Workplace Study*, from the pandemic, "Women in particular have had a negative effect, particularly women of color. They are more likely to have been laid off during the COVID-19 crisis, to stall their jobs, and to jeopardize their financial stability."

Sadly, even when many women's jobs were impacted by the pandemic, some employers showed very little empathy or understanding during these difficult times. They didn't seem to understand that women's job options are so important to their personal and professional achievement, for their long-term financial benefits, and for their stability.

The COVID-19 crisis was an impetus for all of us to think differently about how we work, what work can look like, and what work can feel like. The crisis can help us to rethink and reimagine the future of work.

For example, early in the crisis, we discovered that corporate America and our K-12 education programs are paralyzed by an obsolete employment paradigm and a very conservative education structure. It was obvious that both corporate America and our K-12 education programs needed to reinvest in their own employees because each failed miserably due to of lack of leadership, organizational skills, teamwork, and direction at the beginning of the COVID-19 pandemic and well into 2021. People have been laid off at the fastest pace in history during the crisis. Many workers have been furloughed, and other workers left their jobs because of emotional stress and burnout from being expected to create more with less money. Two other contributing factors to this workplace crisis are employment toxicity and nearly nonexistent leadership and management.

To move forward and make significant changes, whether in the corporate or educational setting, leaders found that we really need to invest in better communicative and collaborative social emotional learning (SEL) skills. It took this crisis for many leaders to understand the value of trusting in the talents of their employees. Their employees were around them all the time, yet many leaders did not grasp the immense ability they had instant access to. They were further unable to perceive this advantage due to the pandemic tension that clouded their lens. This talent is a true differentiator, necessary to succeed and be competitive in a business or educational environment. Sadly, the lack of this understanding caused some to fail completely because of the leaders' poor response to the tragedy of the pandemic.

Analysis has shown that when leaders trust in people and validate their attributes and achievements, they add to the ongoing efforts and success of the team.

Diversity is having a seat at the table. Inclusion is having a voice. Belonging is having that voice be heard.

—Liz Fosslien

"Strong teams are starting with the individual. Individuals who know their talents are working together to shape better alliances, and more thoughtful partnerships are creating stronger teams," wrote the authors of the article "How to Improve Teamwork in the Workplace," published by Gallup in 2021. Dedicated workers who are respected, valued, and given innovative learning experiences to engage their talents through creative ideas, and who have the choice and voice to sit at the decision-making table, will strive to contribute 100 percent to their work. This leadership encourages loyalty to the organization, too.

Great leaders know that team members need open doors, clear communication, and constructive opportunities. When strong leaders lead, invest in their teams, and create a caring, empathetic workforce, they empower their teams to better appreciate the advantages of collaboration. They also build high-performance teams and learn ways to strengthen teamwork. This caliber of leadership offers their teams so many benefits.

Let's look at K-12 education, which is overwhelmingly a female industry. Yet, men hold the superintendencies or admin leadership positions in nearly 14,000 school districts. This figure is particularly grim considering that the talent pool is deep with women. According to government statistics and the findings of a new longitudinal poll, women make up 76 percent of teachers, 52 percent of principals, and 78 percent of school central office managers. Despite this, they account for fewer than a quarter of superintendents, according to a study done in the summer of 2016 by AASA,

the School Superintendents Association. However, this figure reflects an improvement over the previous year, when just 13 percent of the superintendents were female.

What will we women leaders do to shift these numbers and catapult a ready women's labor force to their deserved, prosperous future? We need to guide and model with empathy, intuition, and collaboration.

We are each on this planet for only a short time. Each of us has the responsibility to lead, embody our best selves, and inspire others with intent. I invite you to be an involved participant in this powerful leadership process and learning journey with me. Pull up a chair and sit with me at the leadership table. Let's embark upon a new journey to discover *The Unique Individual You*!

Putting Purpose into Practice

CREATE YOUR VISION BOARD

Vision boards (also called dream boards) are an innovative blend of architecture (because you are literally building a physical board) and visual thinking strategies. They inspire you to think about your life and learning goals, and they help you to develop a roadmap for how to achieve them. A vision board can be a concrete, consistent learning guide that helps keep you focused on your goals. Your vision board's aim is to help you bring your goals to life!

How should you create your vision board? You can use paper sculpture materials and techniques, or you can excite your digital diva by using tech tools and resources. (See page 33 for a curated list of tech tools and resources.)

What should you put on your vision board? The most effective vision boards tap into how you want to feel, not just the material items you want. Include images and words that encourage and motivate you. There are absolutely no rules and no wrong approaches to building your vision board. Consider images of feelings you want to have, places you want to visit, experiences you want to enjoy, and things you want to purchase.

You may wonder: Do vision boards actually work? YES! Vison boards use visualization, which is one of the most effective mental activities you can perform, according to research published in *Psychology Today* and *The Science of Stuff*. The most up-to-date brain-based learning studies from *Psychology Today* conclude that our emotions create the same mental orders as acts. Feeling something affects your brain much in the same way that doing something does. Visualization is the secret to building your creative visionary road map.

You might be asking yourself: *Where do I start? How can I find the vision and intent of my true calling and leadership in life? What kind of formal support framework can I use as a guide? And how do I know if I'm on the right track?*

Learning should be better than chocolate!

Let's break these questions down into bite-sized pieces of snackable content. My personal motto is that learning should be better than chocolate. Breaking these questions down into smaller pieces will really help you plan and concentrate more quickly and effectively on your vision, intentions, and goals.

I use my vision boards to imagine and visually represent what is most important to me both creatively and personally.

To create my vision boards, I use this six-step process.

STEP 1: BRAINSTORM GOALS

Create a list of goals you would like to achieve in the next six-months to a year.

- Include both personal and academic goals, starting small with just one of each.
- Focus on a time frame, such as the end of a quarter, a semester, or the end of the school or business year.

LOOKING FOR MORE VISION BOARD INSPIRATION?

Check out my vision board Google slide deck to guide your design-and-visionary-leadership process.

- Prompt your thinking with these questions:
  - What have you always wanted to learn?
  - What does the end of the school or business year look like?
  - What do you want to accomplish?
  - What books do you want to read?
  - What problems do you want to solve?
  - What's something you struggle with that you would like to overcome?
  - What's something you would like to learn this year?

STEP 2: GATHER IMAGES

Flip through old magazines and cut out beautiful pictures that resonate with you.

- Ask friends, grandparents, or neighbors for magazines they are done using.
- Canva
- Corkulous
- Desygner
- Dream It Alive
- Google Drawings
- Google Jamboard
- Google Slides with Add-ons
- iWish Bucket List
- Microsoft PowerPoint
- Microsoft SWAY
- Padlet
- PiktoChart
- Pinterest
- Subliminal Vision Boards
- Buy some magazines inexpensively at a dollar store or thrift store.
- Half the fun is finding the perfect magazine and having the conversation of what you will be creating that represents your best professional or personal future self!
- You can also create your vision board digitally. Here are some great tools to use to design your vision boards online.
- Find pictures that represent your goals or that inspire you.
- Focus on how the images make you *feel.*
- Encourage originality and creativity that represent *The Unique Individual You*!

- Here are sources of digital copyright-free images.
- Canva Images
- Free Images
- Image Source
- Inspirational Quote Images
- Pexels
- Pixabay
- PixWizard
- Shutterstock Royalty Free
- Unsplash

STEP 3: CHOOSE THE BASE FOR YOUR VISION BOARD

- You need something for the structure of your board. Ideas include:
- A piece of posterboard or cardboard you can hang on a wall
- A picture frame to hang or set on a shelf
- A blank book or journal that you can tuck away in a drawer or carry with you

STEP 4: ARRANGE THE ART INTO A CREATIVE, VISUALLY APPEALING COLLAGE

- Tape or glue the art to the board.
- Use pens, markers, or pencils to add text, shapes, frames, and lines.
- On a digital board, add arrows, emojis, videos, and GIFs.

STEP 5: ADD MOTIVATIONAL WORDS

- Write motivational, affirmation words on your board that represent how you want to feel.
- Add quotes and bold, strong action words to add meaning and purpose to your display.

STEP 6: REFLECT

- Place your vision board where you can see it often.
- Reflect on your vision board progress or challenges every single day.
- Utilize Google Docs, the free Journey journal app, or a gratitude journal to write down your thoughts and supplement your vision board.
- Get support from your besties and video collaboration using FlipGrid or GatherRound to share your vision stories with mentors, colleagues, or friends in a fun and creative way.
- Host a women's master class to learn together and receive real-time feedback from like minds and also different perspectives.

Chapter 3

YOUR LEADERSHIP PURPOSE AND INNER CALLING

Dream and Follow Where Your Innovators' Compass Will Take You

IDENTIFY YOUR LEADERSHIP PURPOSE AND YOUR INNER CALLING

In the seven years since my son's military accident, I have been intentional about the types of jobs that I take on and the presentations that I give. I use a tool called an innovators' compass (see page 48) to precisely evaluate each consulting contract I am offered. It is really important to me that the work I do is significant; that its leadership purpose influences the community, company, organization, or school I am working with; and that it fulfills my leadership purpose and inner calling.

What is a leadership purpose and inner calling, and how do you identify yours? Let's talk about each in turn.

Leadership Purpose

Leadership purpose is as it sounds. What do you hope to achieve by being a leader?

My leadership purpose is servant leadership. Servant leadership is where you concentrate on the needs of others, particularly your teammates, before you address your own needs. You consider the experiences of others, provide them with the resources they need to achieve their job and personal goals, include them in the decision-making process when necessary, and genuinely create a sense of community within your team.

I heavily rely on servant leadership protocols and my innovators' compass to guide my effective facilitation practices. I also use them to follow through on action items, whether I'm working with a K-12 educational organization or a technology corporation.

I have learned a lot from using this servant leadership mindset. It contributes to greater involvement among my peers, and it creates more confidence while fostering deeper relationships with team members. So, I am all for it. The greatest bonus to servant leadership that I have seen is that it contributes to increased creativity.

If a leader can inspire people with an uplifting work environment, the magic really happens! The artistic capacity of each teammate is unlocked, along with integrity and reason.

Learning is two-fold for me. The two benefits of leadership that I most enjoy are that it provides both a learning perspective and a leadership perspective. As an educator, I obtain fresh critical perspectives, and I am more motivated to lead with an educational, innovative mindset. This is when the learning is really better than chocolate!

What is your leadership purpose? Your leadership purpose does not just appear immediately after you get a job in a leadership role. Nor do you discover your leadership purpose after a good night's rest. Each of us has a leadership purpose that's innately contained and profoundly grounded within us. You need to awaken yours.

WANT TO LEARN MORE ABOUT SERVANT LEADERSHIP?

Visit these sites for information and analysis.

Identifying your leadership purpose can take time. In some cases, it can even take years of following your creative and passion-based learning opportunities before you are able to discover your leadership purpose. Often it takes a hands-on learning experience to heighten our senses, or a chance to discover a new area of concern through a happy learning accident. Or an encounter or leadership discussion with a powerful woman trainer could help you pause and catch your focus.

My leadership purpose was awakened during my undergraduate liberal arts studies at Viterbo University, in La Crosse, Wisconsin, from 1995 to 1999. One of the foundational pillars of my Bachelor of Science and Elementary Education degree was servant leadership—the value of placing others first and working as a collaborative team. I found it fascinating that our education program included this emphasis on servant leadership. I didn't know it at the time, but it would prepare me for my personal and professional future.

VITERBO
UNIVERSITY

To this day, servant leadership guides every decision I make with each human interaction I have. I always aim to lead with purpose, integrity, and compassion. Using a servant leadership model also provides me the opportunity to lead using impartial and respectful learning methods. I appreciate the opportunity to impact educators, business leaders, and students around the world with an educational lens focused on ethical servant leadership.

I choose to lead and have a lasting positive effect on the lives of people I meet and work with on a daily basis. The greatest gift I can provide is my positive, creative genius—the positivity and creativity I bring to my work and those around me. I use this psychological trait to influence others personally and professionally through leadership learning experiences. This gift gives rise to positivity and pleasure in one's life, and it affects and resonates with others. My positive genius has enabled me to carry out and leave a legacy of good for others, through the sharing of stories of hope and optimism that have transformed my perspective from the life-changing events I have experienced—from my youngest son's military accident in 2014 to working with educators and business leaders from around the world.

These purposeful interactions have given me the chance to travel and to learn about other cultures. I am always surprised how similar their teaching, learning, and leadership experiences (including the needs and challenges) are to ours in the United States.

These leadership interactions have also provided me with opportunities to effectively lead and change the way an organization "thinks"—its very culture. Then I can scale a working plan to refocus the organization to value relationships as their top priority.

Every interaction that we have, whether accidental or purposeful, provides us with an active listening opportunity to acquire new insights from the points of view of others. These impressions teach our big beautiful brains to appreciate new insights. They also instill deeper sensitivity and empathic abilities to better understand each other and our world. Here's how to identify your leadership purpose.

- Deeply reflect into your life to understand what influenced you and what type of leadership makes you the most happy.
- Describe your desired leadership impact and legacy.
- Work with a coach, mentor, or peers.
- Define your goals and objectives.

QUESTIONS TO FIND YOUR LEADERSHIP PURPOSE

Professional interests: What stimulates your big beautiful brain without feeling like work?

Personal interests: What piques your insatiable curiosity?

Action related: What types of job tasks or hands-on activity give you the most joy?

Work related: Do you have a work-related cause that you are truly passionate about?

- Make your goals and objectives visible, such as with a vision board.
- Evaluate your progress and map out your next steps through a daily reflection journal. Assess your progress and plan your future actions with purposeful next steps.

Inner Calling

Your inner calling is your passion, your drive. It's what you want to contribute to your leadership world, and to the greater world. With every human experience and conversation, we discover our inner calling to lead our personal and professional lives. As a leader, you want to help others find their own calling, which is so fulfilling in life.

My own inner calling was found in the human experiences I had with others. I asked, *What is my purpose, what is my why, and what and how do I want to contribute? How can I leave my legacy so that my leadership impression can carry on to help others?*

Ask yourself how you can help model the next generation of women leaders. That's how to find your own inner calling. If you're a driven leader, you want to find a solution that helps to build a stronger community of leaders. You want to ensure the purposeful outcomes will impact the greater society and our world.

Using your vision board can help you to find your inner calling. What images are you drawn to?

Your personal relationships can help you to find your inner calling. When you're working with others, consider what makes you happiest. Ask yourself, *If I'm this happy now with this project, is there a type of work I could pursue to put this into practice?*

~

Take a moment to think about where you are in your leadership journey. Consider the influences of people, places, and experiences that have contributed to your career so far. It's important to have a long, heartfelt conversation with yourself and answer the following questions to better understand your ambitious life map and visualize your best future self.

- What interactions have you experienced that contributed to or influenced a personal interest or passion project?
- What leadership guidance did those people provide to help you pursue that dream?
- Which particular people have especially influenced and mentored you to guide your leadership purpose?
- Where do you see your best self as a leader in the next six months? In the next year? In the next three years?
- What is your current inner leadership calling, passion, or purpose?
- What three words best describe your current leadership style?
- Why is your leadership style so important to you?
- How do you model your leadership vision in your organization?
- What three words would you like to describe your leadership style a year from now?
- What drives you to seek more information to invest in yourself as a transformational leader, and why?
- Does your current leadership influence resonate with others? If so, how do you know this to be true? (Share an example.)
- What do you need to change professionally to influence others?
- How do you model and build creative leadership confidence in other future women leaders?
- What three strategies from this chapter will you put into practice and model to navigate your visionary roadmap with leadership purpose?

INVEST IN INNER WORK

When I ask myself the questions posed above, I wonder, *If I invest in myself and do my inner work, will that unlock my leadership potential for my outer work?*

On his last day of employment at General Electric Corporation, former CEO Jeffrey R. Immelt noted, "Leadership is this intense journey into yourself." His message was clear: Effective leadership doesn't necessarily equate with output. It's much bigger and much more personal.

I believe our current educational and business conversations miss acknowledging that the greatest opportunity for change isn't in cloud computing, offshoring jobs, upgrading internal employee communication tools, or optimizing supply chains. All of these changes are external and extrinsic. They ignore what Immelt was talking about: Leadership and work at their core are personalized learning experiences.

I believe that what we conceive of as "work" is nearly entirely our "outer work." The opportunity to personalize our inner work and to personalize our learning experiences is usually absent from our current job experiences. Yet the time and energy we spend on self-development, self-awareness, and self-worth add to the success and longevity of our "outer work." This "inner work" will make you more aware of what's most important in your life and help you hone in on your leadership purpose while helping you envision your leadership visionary roadmap. As a bonus, it is valuable that you are putting yourself first and investing in real life skills as you find your leadership purpose.

We need to start prioritizing ourselves with our inner work. I know it can be daunting, especially when you have too many things on your to-do list. I think many of us don't know how to incorporate mindfulness into our work hours. Even if investing in your inner work seems counterintuitive, it can have substantial benefits for both your work and home life. Here are a few examples.

- Prioritizing well-being is something most of us need to practice, but with focus, we can all have more fulfilling, productive workdays.
- Changing our daily habits at work to value well-being and balance has been shown to foster more positive feelings both at work and at home.
- Simply increasing awareness of our experiences and reflection habits can make a big difference in how we feel at work, interact with our coworkers, and do our work.

LOOKING FOR MORE VISION BOARD INSPIRATION?

For more information on how to find meaning and purpose in your work, visit "Meaning and Purpose at Work" from the Better Up leadership organization.

Developing your leadership skills and empathy are major drivers to pursue your inner calling and professional leadership passions. When you are more aware and in control of your inner and outer work experiences, you are also contributing to better work-life-family balance. Further research shows a significant link between investing in personalized inner work and finding meaning or purpose through your actual job, too.

The Umbrella Effect

A story from my life illustrates the importance of doing inner work to support outer work.

In the fall of 2015, I was invited by Russel Tarr, an inspirational educational leader from France who created Class Tools and coordinates the Practical Pedagogies conference, to give a presentation at their annual conference to be hosted in Toulouse, France. I was thrilled by the request Russel had made and the opportunity it afforded me to network and learn with European educators to gain new teaching and learning perspectives.

But it would be a long trip that would take me away from my home and family for several weeks. It had been 18 months since Jacob's accident. I wondered if it was safe for him to go or if I could go alone.

I listened to my leadership heart and my educator gut as I pursued my dreams and intentionally followed my innovators' compass.

I decided to go, and to this day, the experience has left an impact and impression on me. I had so many conversations with European educational leaders. That experience taught me the importance of prioritizing a learning moment by being present and allowing myself to truly enjoy meaningful conversations with others.

At that time, Jacob was still wheelchair bound 50 percent of the time and it was difficult for him to walk independently. I knew that navigating a European trip with a wheelchair and my son's disabilities would present us with new and unique challenges, especially if some of the venues were not accessible or ADA compliant.

Yet I wanted to afford my family with a new learning experience, and I longed to have a new travel adventure. Jeff and I discussed this opportunity at length, and we decided we needed to move forward, push ourselves to experience life again, and travel in new ways. It would just be different. We decided this would be our new normal to acclimate to the "different" environments and experiences of traveling with an adult child who had many disabilities.

Lots of planning needed to take place, and lots of research needed to be done so we could successfully travel across the European countryside. We were up for this challenge, and Russel helped guide us through the accessibilities questions we posed for him regarding the venue, hotel, and outdoor adventure travels.

The traveling experience with Jacob went more seamlessly than we anticipated, and it did not cause any major setbacks. It took more patience and time than we were used to at home to navigate the wheelchair ramps, elevators, and transportation vehicles. Yet it was all very similar to what we were already doing at home, just in a different place. As a family, we were learning new ways to enjoy life and travel once again. Knowing that I could give my son these types of new learning experiences and a sense of independence filled my heart with gratitude.

The opportunity to present at the Practical Pedagogies conference had been on my bucket list for a long time. I had been an avid Twitter follower of Russel's for more than a decade. To have the opportunity to present at his event and personally learn with him and his colleagues was one of my life's greatest moments.

I was so impressed with Russel's organization and the workflow of the conference. His attention to detail was so similar to mine. I had the opportunity to present multiple sessions, and I was afforded the opportunity to learn from other educational leaders who attended from throughout Europe. My learning bucket was overflowing with new knowledge and inspirational ideas. I could not wait to bring it back to our technology leadership workshops!

What most impressed me at this particular conference was the depth and magnitude of the conversations that took place among the attendees. The conversations were infused with design thinking and hexagonal thinking strategies and concepts for us to use to solve challenging problems as a collaborative global team. Design thinking and hexagonal thinking are iterative processes in which we aim to understand the user, challenge assumptions, and reframe issues in order to find alternate methods and solutions that may not be immediately obvious based on our initial level of understanding. This enables us to monitor the target user and to build empathy by examining the problem, questioning the assumptions, and questioning the ramifications.

So, we asked: What is the overall learning outcome we wanted to achieve from the learning challenge that we were provided: making a cup of tea? The example problem they gave us was to find the most efficient way to make tea and keep it hot. We then were challenged to apply that type of thinking to the classroom or our leadership styles to improve the overall learning outcome. I was challenged for the first time in a long time to think critically, problem solve, and be more aware of my interactions with others. I was again in the seat of an active learner, and I had longed for these types of new experiences!

Another thing I noticed is that most attendees were not reliant upon their mobile devices. They were present, vigilant, active participants in learning conversations with others. My reading of the room and my observation skills caught on to this right away. It was a pleasant relief to set down my tech devices and observe and enjoy the wholesomeness of these creative learning moments. I felt so free, at ease, and extremely comfortable with all of my new educator friends. I relished the opportunity to learn with a collaborative team.

The conference lasted for two amazing days and two evenings in Toulouse, including celebratory dinners together each night. After the conference ended, my family and I stayed an extra five days. We ventured out on our own to discover a little bit more of Toulouse, continued onward to explore the countryside to the Mediterranean Sea, and then we went on to the French Riviera of Nice and Monaco.

As we explored the city of Toulouse, my main priority was to experience the Umbrella Skyline Impact Project. The skylines of some of the streets in Toulouse were filled with cascading umbrellas, creating a canopy of rich, vibrant colors.

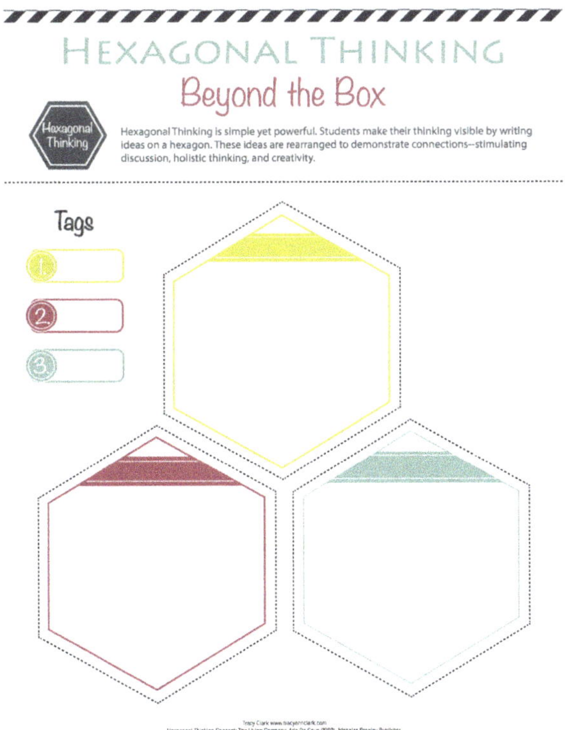

The Umbrella Project was born in Águeda, Portugal, in 2012, and it quickly spread throughout the world. It was definitely a must-see for me and my family! The motto of this project is to color life. It brings color to the gray spaces of the city, and it provides joyful experiences that may result in tear-filled, smiling faces on those who pass by! It's a simple, unusual idea that brings life and protection to public spaces.

Seeing the Umbrella Project left a calming effect on me, providing a safety net of comfort and joy. I was filled with awe. As a family, we found it to be one of the most breathtaking moments of our lives. As I gazed at it, I knew this inner feeling of peace, happiness, and gratitude must be replicated and prioritized in order for me to continue to invest in my inner work, so I could represent my best self and leadership influence in my outer work.

Prioritizing well-being and choosing happiness is a talent. Research has proven that it is a collection of skills that can be taught to both children and adults. It's not simply autonomy, grit, or mindfulness. Each skill contributes to a well-being umbrella that shields us from life's storms, helps us find meaning in our experiences, and is highly predictive of future success.

Many of us have faced numerous challenges and setbacks in our lives, and we can think of these as our rainy days. Sometimes we have little influence over these parts of our lives, just as we have little influence over the weather.

Life isn't always bright, and we waste a lot of energy wishing the storm clouds would just go away rather than adequately shielding ourselves from the rain. The good news is that we all have umbrellas, though some are large, some are little, some have holes, and others are forgotten in our closets.

Your umbrella is made up of emotional and cognitive intelligences and qualities such as gratitude, empathy, resilience, and purpose. These qualities are shared by the happiest and most successful people and can be used to predict future happiness.

We can strengthen our umbrellas and begin to reframe the issues we face by employing our umbrella talents. All of these abilities are crucial and work best when used together to reduce what seemed like a tornado to a gentle rain. Working hard day after day with grit is admirable, but without a sense of purpose, it is meaningless. As our umbrella grows in size, healthy behaviors are essential for providing the strength needed to keep it up, especially when the large storms come through. Using our umbrella provides us with the courage to aggressively seek life's possibilities, regardless of the weather or the storms that have passed. We might even discover some puddles to play in, even in the aftermath of the worst storms.

When we were young, we relied on other people to hold the umbrellas to protect us. But as we become older and venture out on our own, we need to use our own umbrellas. Having your own umbrella is liberating. Relying on the umbrellas of others leaves our safety in their hands.

Everyone in a strong and confident group has their own umbrella, so when you need some additional cover and support, there's plenty to go around. Other people are more likely to use their umbrellas after seeing how you use yours. It's a chain reaction, and the best way to teach umbrella talents is to set an example by using your own.

By now, you've probably realized the significance of my book's graphic cover. I'm hoping the umbrella effect inspires you to leave a lasting positive memory, while serving as a friendly reminder to invest in yourself and your personal well-being, to lead with purpose, and to prioritize your happiness as you embark on your new leadership journey.

Putting Purpose into Practice

IDENTIFY YOUR LEADERSHIP GOALS WITH THE INNOVATORS' COMPASS

My leadership story illustrates how a person can discover and follow a leadership calling. But what do you hope to do in your lifetime to leave a legacy of good? How are you going to follow your leadership roadmap to reach your goals?

I use a unique tool called the Innovators' Compass. It helps me to navigate my visionary road map and overcome the hiccups, bumps, and struggles that are thrown at me unexpectedly.

I need to give a huge shoutout to Ela Ben-Ur, the creator of the Innovators' Compass and her supportive website *https://innovatorscompass.org,* who is excited about having people of all ages express and amplify their natural forms of doing things better. Since 2012, she has collaborated extensively with educators and organizations involved in design thinking.

Ela worked with the famous innovation company IDEO for 13 years. Her design experience and leadership at IDEO spanned a wide range of markets, locations, and sectors. She joined coaching teams, facilitated clients, and cofounded IDEO's Leadership Lab to cultivate project leaders.

Since 2007, Ela has taught courses from product design to life design at the groundbreaking Olin College of Engineering. She has led workshops at venues including MIT (her alma mater), SXSW EDU, the National Science Teachers' Association, AIGA, the International Development Architecture Summit, and the US AIDS Conference. She credits her daughters as her inspiration.

The Innovators' Compass is a free tool to help you get unstuck when you need to solve a problem, help you visualize with purpose, and coordinate and prioritize your thoughts and analytical approach to meet a goal.

To use the Innovators' Compass to solve a problem with purpose, first ask yourself these five questions:

1. **People:** Who's involved?
2. **Observations:** What's happening?
3. **Principles:** What matters most?
4. **Ideas:** What ways are there?
5. **Experiments:** What's a step to try?

The Innovators' Compass identifies five viewpoints (people, observations, principles, ideas, and experiments) that nurture your key women-in-leadership neuroscience strengths of empathy, intuition, and collaboration when you are solving a problem.

Review the Innovators' Compass graphic below and read the five questions to gain perspective on how you can visualize and navigate your leadership roadmap. It will help you attain your future leadership goals as an individual, yet this activity is so much more engaging within a collaborative team. A team approach is where we actively listen to all ideas that are shared, and we can learn and empathize with others through multiple viewpoints and voices to make deeper learning connections.

Here's an example of how I've used the Innovators' Compass. When COVID-19 hit, we had to move our face-to-face K-12 classes online. We needed to find the best fit for our K-12 educators to actively participate in this new type of learning experience. I used the Innovators' Compass to make our online classes and coursework more student-centered, so they were more engaging and motivating for all teachers as new learners, regardless of their technology skill level.

1. **People:** Elementary teachers: I need to identify the concept aligned to the technology skill and then consider the type of outcome we're looking for to make a learning impact with students.
2. **Observations:** Research what we know that's currently working and what's not working with online learning among teachers who have little to no experience teaching online.

3. **Principles:** Ask what matters most: What we've learned from the research is that when learning something new, it's important to break it into small, engaging chunks of information that are rich in visuals, include auditory elements, and are complemented with text to meet the varied learning styles of the teachers. We have to model what we are expecting of the teachers to model to the students.
4. **Ideas:** From the principles we've gathered, we list all of the ways we could design the course. We will use small activities to help teachers engage with the learning so they can see, feel, and connect with the emotion of how this type of learning is different and how teachers can use it to interact with the students in their classrooms. At the same time, this active hands-on participation as a learner builds the teachers' learning confidence.
5. **Experiments:** This is when we build the coursework out and test it with teachers who are willing to try it and provide critical feedback: what's working, what's not working, what they liked, and what they would change.

Let's put your purpose into practice and see how the Innovators' Compass can support your efforts to solve a problem, get unstuck, or achieve a goal. It will help you to reflect on the person you currently are and the person you want to become to lead your visionary roadmap in life.

Chapter 4

MAKE THE LEADERSHIP EXPERIENCE TRANSFORMATIONAL

Visualize Your Best Self Each and Every Day

CHILDHOOD AND LIFETIME EXPERIENCES DEFINE YOUR LEADERSHIP STYLE

We are all shaped and defined by our experiences, beginning in childhood. My first leadership influences were my family and my life growing up in northeast Iowa on a dairy farm. My childhood gave me the opportunity to think about the value of hard work and how responsibility affects productivity. I am very grateful to my dad, Jack Hemesath, for giving me, at a very young age, hands-on farming experience to give my big beautiful brain many different learning opportunities that stimulated and enriched my love of learning in the field of STEM (science, technology, engineering, mathematics).

It's said, "Like father, like son," but in my family's case the saying is, "Like mother, like son," because my paternal grandma, Iola Hemesath, helped raise me. In the process, she kindled my love and enthusiasm for STEM. Also cooking, baking, and even gardening. She did this all while running a business. My grandma Iola owned a catering company, and she served full-course meals at local weddings, funerals, and celebratory events.

This is where I first discovered the significance of quality leadership. From my grandma, I learned that one needs to communicate effectively, listen actively, and be an outstanding customer service agent—all at the same time. My grandmother exhibited these traits time and time again without hesitation.

The quality time I spent with my grandmother making delicious and stunning food developed my creative and design presentation skills. Little did I know at the time that my grandma was an outstanding woman influencer and leadership role model. She trained me in vital life and business skills to prepare me for my own business career and success.

I prefer to take the path less traveled. I began my adult life by becoming a mother to three boys first, greatly assisted by my husband, Jeff, and then I proceeded to pursue my four-year degree in elementary education at Viterbo University. I got my first teaching job at Bangor Elementary School in Wisconsin, where I also did my first teaching practicum and worked with an amazing team of inspirational female educators who were my first educational mentors. These amazing ladies helped me craft and enhance my teaching and learning skills with students of every ability, and they provided me an opportunity to lead with tech-infused lessons and activities. They also modeled active listening, patience, and learning effectiveness. As a bonus, they taught me when to lean in to meaningful conversations and when to listen with empathy and respond with compassion to invest in our students. This is when I discovered the educational, social, and emotional impacts a teacher can have on a student for a lifetime.

A very special thank you goes to Leota, Sonja, Nan, and Kristen, who were my first women teacher mentors at Bangor Elementary School. They believed in me and all of my crazy tech-enhanced lessons. They let me lead and pursue my educational leadership passions, and they supported my efforts with critical feedback for improvements and celebrations for a job well done.

After five years of teaching at Bangor Elementary, I was eager for more learning, so I decided to pursue my Master of EdTech and Professional Learning Communities. I accepted a new job as the EdTech director at the regional service agency, leading and teaching K-12 educators and administrators.

This is where I discovered my passion for designing, implementing, and leading vocational and STEM learning projects with K-12 educators. This is also where I met my first woman mentor in EdTech leadership and curriculum design. Myrna Daugherty helped me build my leadership confidence and speaking influence. She helped me become more aware of my idiosyncrasies, like the "umms and ands" I used as verbal fillers and that many of us rely on when we are anxious or nervous. She helped me to understand the essential gift of quiet pausing without saying a word. This technique allows an individual to reclaim one's thoughts, take a breath to calm oneself, ensure the next spoken words will make an impact without appearing nervous or unprepared, and drive home the message on the topic.

Myrna was also an excellent writer, a grammar and wordsmith queen, who helped me improve my writing style and my visual media presentation skills, too. She was patient and kind. She encouraged me to take risks, yet she offered me timely, constructive feedback to improve my leadership style and influence with others. Yes indeed, Myrna was an active role model and mentor to me. She provided me with the access and equity to resources and role-modeling learning experiences that changed and advanced my career, by her influence as a compassionate women leader.

I am also very grateful to a male role model in my life from this same agency. Jerry Freimark was the administrator at the time I was first hired. He could see my learning potential, my dedicated work ethic, my drive, my visionary mindset, and the way I interacted with people and the projects I delivered. He believed in me, and he invested in my leadership capabilities as a woman educator.

Jerry also provided me with critical insight and knowledge of what quality customer service looks and feels like. Even though we were a K-12 educational organization, I found out immediately that we must lead with an effective business influence and model with a resilient mindset to improve and impact teacher-leaders in western Wisconsin. We needed to consistently lead with integrity and passion-driven perseverance, and to actively listen to our customers' needs—our K-12 educators, administrators, and students within these school districts.

~

What success looked like in this job was reflected in the how and why we provided effective transformational teaching and learning services. It was imperative that high-quality and effective K-12 educational programs were designed, led, and implemented with purpose to meet the diverse needs of the 26 school districts in western Wisconsin. Yes, the job demands were significant. Yet I was up for the challenge, and I enjoyed working with a team of brilliant, creative women and being supported by a male administrative leader.

I was disheartened when Jerry retired from the regional agency after five years. Yet change is inevitable to move forward and make progress. A new administrator was brought on board within six months of Jerry's retirement announcement. This new male administrator proved to be the most difficult adversary I would face, but the experience did help advance my career.

After seven years as an EdTech director within this service agency, two years after Jerry retired, Myrna moved on to finish her career as a curriculum director within a local school district. At that point, I felt something was lacking in my career. At times, a sense of unhappiness infiltrated my days, challenging work conversations that were often one-sided took place, and my work environment was no longer filling me with joy. It consumed me with unfulfilling "outer work" and my purposeful "inner work" had to take a back seat, or so I thought. I pushed to get through the massive workloads that I was now assigned from the new administrator. His priorities were so different from mine.

He lacked the quality leadership traits of a servant leader. This guy did not understand the purpose of outer work and inner work analysis: to define one's leadership balance. Nor did he grasp the purpose of how one contributes to gratifying work that is personalized to represent one's best self in a leadership position.

More information will follow on this drama-filled leadership storyline in Chapter 5, yet I want to fast-forward this story to share with you what was truly bothering me and contributing to my underlying unhappiness. I also want to emphasize the importance of how a leader can influence and motivate others by modeling effective leadership conversations, which can transform and change lives.

This new administrator was a thorn in my side, and I also had many personal family issues going on at the same time. My father had been diagnosed with pancreatic cancer, and the prognosis was not good. He shared his ill-fated hunch at Christmas in 2007.

"I think the cancer has caught me," my dad said.

We were all shocked, and he proceeded to tell us that he had not been feeling very well for three months. In February 2008, an endocrinologist confirmed his fate. The cancer had spread so quickly that my dad had only 6 to 12 months to live.

Over the next nine months, I had the opportunity to spend more quality time and enjoy conversations with my father on weekends when I could get away from work. During our talks, my father motivated me to confront my feelings of discontentment at work. I knew I had to either try my best to get along with the new administrator while standing up for my leadership beliefs and standards, which meant butting heads with him on a daily basis, or I needed to walk away. My dad actively listened to me and my struggles. He could read the fatigue in my body language. My head was hanging low, and my shoulders drooped as I sat next to him in his easy chair in the kitchen.

My dad could see I was tired, burned out, and utterly disgusted with the situation I was in. He shared his leadership guidance and encouragement.

"Have you thought of starting your own professional development business?" my dad asked. "It appears to me there may be a high need and value for the services you could provide schools."

He could see I perked up and lifted my head to look at him with a smile.

"Could I quit my job and start my own business?" I asked. "Who would take care of all the schools I provide professional learning, in-person services, and workshops for?"

A million questions filled my mind, the "What if's?" and "How might I's?" We discussed business topics and implementation strategies for the next hour as my dad grew tired. I knew the conversation was too much for him. Most likely, my enthusiasm wore him out as well. The cancer and treatment made him so weak. I thanked him for his time, business leadership insights, and entrepreneurship wisdom. My dad spent 50 years running a 400-acre dairy, hog, and crop farm, and he had an incredible wealth of knowledge to share. If I only had taken more time to invest in these types of conversations when I was younger, instead of waiting until I was 40 years old. During such a trying moment in our lives, I would have realized much earlier the importance and relevance of prioritizing these life-giving and memory-making moments more often.

I left that day's visit beaming with ideas and more learning confidence than at any other time in my life. The possibilities of work and opportunities suddenly seemed endless. I enjoyed the two-hour car ride back to my home in Brownsville, Minnesota, dreaming of the future.

My father passed away on October 22, 2008, surrounded by my mom and most of my siblings. I remember sleeping on the couch in the adjacent room and being abruptly awoken by a feeling of warmth on my arm and cheek at 2:58 a.m. I woke up, looked around, and went to check on my father in his makeshift hospital room in our family room. I touched his hand and gently spoke to him. His hand was warm, yet I could tell he was no longer breathing.

My father provided me with one of the greatest gifts in my lifetime through his leadership encouragement and guidance. I knew that he believed in me. To this day, some nights I wake up around 2:58 a.m. to that same warm feeling on my arm and cheek. These subtle interactions remind me that my father is still looking out for me and guiding me with his presence.

I wish my dad could have been there when I took the leap of faith and started Innovative Educator Consulting Corporation in January 2009.

Little did I realize how busy I would become within the first year of running my EdTech women-in-leadership corporation. I soon began wishing I could clone myself so I could fulfill all the professional learning requests that were coming in. Within the first 12 months, I started assembling a team, largely recruited from teachers and EdTech coordinators whom I had met and considered "game changers" in their teaching and learning fields, and from the professional relationships I had formed in the arena of technology integration.

Dan and Sally King were my first employees back in 2009 through 2014. I was so grateful to have them both onboard because they were just retiring from teaching positions as a technology integration specialist and speech pathologist. Both Dan and Sally had many years of creditable teaching experiences and creative technology talents to help support my company. Hiring them allowed me to expand our professional learning services. As a collaborative team effort, we provided the first 1:1 iPad trainings and implementations in the state of Wisconsin, while addressing and meeting the many diverse needs of teachers and students as new learners with this type of mobile technology. We were highly successful as a collaborative team!

By 2012, as more professional learning requests came in, I needed to expand our team, this time with a focus on women-in-educational-technology leadership. I hired Deb Norton, Velvet Homes, and Mariah Richards as part-time EdTech consultants. This created my team of professional women leaders, all of whom have extensive experience with teaching students and adult learners in the classroom, and are highly respected in their fields with technology integration.

As part of our Innovative Educator Consulting team, Deb, Velvet, and Mariah have an equitable say in the decisions we make and in the creative content we design and deliver. In return, I could now receive critical, genuine, timely, and honest feedback from these talented women, which helped promote the continued success and creative visionary leadership roadmap of our EdTech leadership services.

The things you are passionate about are not random. They are your true calling in life to find your purpose.

When 2014 rolled around, I learned that a multimillion-dollar EdTech corporations was eyeing up my company. They were interested in the amount of professional learning services and business contracts we were delivering throughout the Midwest and expanding nationally and globally. This company inquired about the inner workings of our business leadership model and the professional learning services we offered K-12 organizations. Within a month of our first informal meetings, we were invited to several roundtable meetings and collaborative conversations with business stakeholders and a few of their leadership team members.

Then the EdTech company asked to acquire my Innovative Educator Consulting Corporation, offering to pay up to tenfold of the value of my business.

I was overwhelmed at the thought of selling my company to an EdTech giant. They wanted me to stay on in a full-time salaried position to run and lead their new EdTech leadership services, affiliated with my company name, and hire my own team to cover a seven-state region of professional development services.

I thought, *this would mean I would give up my rights and ownership to my company, and I would once again be working for an employer and not calling my own shots.*

Several more meetings took place with this EdTech company. We were not finding a happy medium on the final fair value price of my company and my salary and employment compensation package. I needed to take a weeklong break from negotiations to evaluate my options and decide if this was the best decision for me, my company, and my family.

That one week made a world of difference. That was the week I received the phone call informing me of Jacob's accident.

All business negotiations came to a standstill. Days turned into weeks, and weeks turned into months. The EdTech company looking to acquire my company could not wait anymore, and they moved on without Innovative Educator Consulting Corporation. At that time, what was most important was my focus on and dedication to my son and his recovery. I knew in my head and heart that everything would be okay, and I would continue to lead Innovative Educator Consulting Corporation with even more honor and strength.

Today, Innovative Educator Consulting Corporation has grown into a global EdTech leadership company, representing a team of 14 dynamic, imaginative, creative, talented Midwestern women master educators. They are my inspirational guides as they motivate me with new ideas and model mentorship strategies with students and teachers. I cannot thank them enough for their time, effort, creative energy, and professional consultancy services to best represent Innovative Educator Consulting Corporation. Another special thanks to Deb and Velvet as my educational leaders in the Midwest and additional teacher leaders Valerie, Stacci, Angie, Maria, Mariah, Kristin, Kathleen, Helen, Monica, Rebecca, Sonja, and Vanessa for being part of my incredible women-in-leadership team! #TogetherWeAreBetter

By now, you may have recognized the purpose of my leadership story and the reason why servant leadership is my inner calling. Every human interaction wasn't accidental. It was purposefully orchestrated as part of my career and life plan, even though I didn't know it and may not have seen it from the vantage point at the time. Each of these new teaching partnerships has given me teaching and life lessons that are important to experience. Through them, I have learned new, culturally diverse viewpoints, which have strengthened my entrepreneurial leadership skills and business mentality. That is why I feel it is critical to give back to our community of leaders and learners, particularly our future women leaders, so that they, too, may continue the humanitarian message of leaving a positive legacy for future generations. I will still strive to lead by example and continue to plant the talents of servant leadership and nurture the personal and professional satisfaction known as our positive genius. Most importantly, I will be a change agent to make a difference as a woman role model and a global influencer. I will share my vision of empowerment, hope, and inspiration with future women leaders with compassion, honesty, and servant leadership.

I've shared how my childhood and lifetime experiences defined my leadership style. Now it's your turn. How did your childhood and lifetime experiences define your leadership style? What new experiences can you seek to further refine your leadership style?

LEADERSHIP HABITS AND ROUTINES

Research suggests that it takes an average of 30 days for a new habit to become automatic.

I have discovered in my life, especially in the past 20 years running my leadership company, that if I form a new routine, it is really a series of habits, such as eating healthier by following a food plan, carrying out a dedicated task to improve my productivity, or implementing a new leadership practice to influence others. It takes daily dedication for a month or even two to allow my actions to become regular habits of mind.

What habit or ritual would you like to develop in the next 30 days?

What tactics do you need to pursue to make this new pattern a habit in your life?

Would you want to invite or partner or teammate to inspire you to feel more successful?

When you believe in yourself and pursue purposeful learning, you prioritize yourself. You put yourself in the driver's seat. You are also making new neuronal learning pathways in your big beautiful brain, as you create and reinforce electrical dendrite signals in your brain. Think of dendrites as similar to transistors in a device, conducting basic operation using electrical signals. Dendrites accept feedback from several other neurons and pass these inputs to the cell body. If excited enough, the neuron creates an action potential—an electrical response that activates other neurons. Wide networks of these neurons interact with each other to produce thoughts and actions.

New learning opportunities strengthen the memory of the brain with positive and negative learning stimuli and react accordingly. This current learning behavior of a habit or a ritual specifically affects the positive and negative stimuli in the brain's neurons, which will impact your social emotional learning responses and your communicative and physical relationships with others. The bonus of all this, though, is that your brain provides you with instantaneous, rewarding memories from these new activities. Your brain longs for more electrical neuron action potential to keep repeating and triggering satisfied learning experiences.

In effect, this is why we carry out everyday habits with purpose. Indeed, our habits are incredibly necessary to shape new patterns, which, in exchange, reward our big beautiful brains with the quest for new experiences. These neuronal experiences keep our minds busy and vibrant, while continuing to persevere, carry out projects, and accomplish our goals, as our life and visionary roadmap prepares us for an unknown future.

Lifelong learning (aka, upskilling) is one aspect of the solution. What it means is giving our employees opportunities to gain the knowledge, tools, and ability they need to use advanced and ever-changing workplace and technologies skills in their daily lives.

When you believe in yourself and welcome a friend along your transformational path, you are more likely to excel in the challenge at hand. Why? According to Gallup, people who have a best friend at work are seven times more likely to be involved in their work, perform assignments, and spend time together outside of work doing fitness and well-being activities. Gallup also found that people who have a good friend at work are more likely to be happy. What's more, strong working friendships are tied to higher customer engagement and improved profits for the company.

Developing habits and routines can be fun when the process is shared with a friend, colleague, or loved one. If you find yourself breaking the promises you made to yourself, or lapsing in the new habits that you are working on, ask a friend to join you on this new path. Two creative minds are stronger than one. You can encourage and inspire each other and hold each other accountable. It can also increase your achievement and help you develop lifetime learning patterns to more consistently balance work-life-family.

Some leadership habits I have developed over the past 10 years are drinking water, taking Pomodoro breaks, walking, gratitude journaling, watching inspiring Ted Talks, enjoying essential oils, and cooking heart-healthy foods.

Drinking Water

I start each day by drinking two 16-ounce glasses of water. Our big beautiful brains are 80 percent water. We need water to feed and nourish our brains so that we can stay hydrated and do our best creative work. I always keep a glass of water with me and make sure I drink at least 100 ounces a day.

Taking Pomodoro Breaks

When working long hours creating content on my computer, I remind myself to get up every hour from my desk by setting a transitional digital timer called the Pomodoro Technique Timer.

The Pomodoro Technique is a time management strategy that can help you achieve more in less time. The technique was developed in the late 1980s by then-university-student Francesco Cirillo, who was struggling to focus on his studies and complete assignments. Feeling overwhelmed, he asked himself to commit to just 10 minutes of focused study time. Encouraged by the challenge, he found a kitchen timer shaped like a tomato ("pomodoro" in Italian), and the Pomodoro Technique was born. Its biggest strength is its simplicity.

1. Write a to-do list and get a timer.
2. Set your timer for 25 minutes and focus on a single task until the timer rings. (Even though Francesco used 10 minutes, teachers have adapted this to 25 minutes, followed by a 5-minute break.)
3. When your session ends, write "one Pomodoro completed!" and cross off your to-do list what you completed.
4. Enjoy a five-minute break.
5. After four Pomodoros, take a longer, more restorative 15- to 30-minute break.

During my breaks, I take 10- to 20-minute power walks, drink water, and clean my home, using a list of small, household cleaning tasks—such as sweeping, vacuuming, mopping, or doing laundry. It's surprising how much household cleaning can be done in 10 to 20 minutes. Plus, when I know I have only 10 to 20 minutes to work, I can stay focused and energized. Bonus: Some days I get 60+ minutes of walking, exceeding the American Heart Association's guidelines. My heart, big beautiful brain, and body love me for it.

Walking

As I mentioned, I often spend my breaks walking. According to an article from *Think Health*, walking briskly for 20 minutes a day offers many health benefits. These include protecting your heart, losing a few pounds, sharpening your memory, changing your attitude, and even sleeping better!

Plus, according to a report published in *The Proceedings of the National Academy of Sciences*, the hippocampus of our great big beautiful brains starts to shrink as we age, generally starting around age 55 or 60. However, researchers made an interesting discovery when they took brain scans of study participants who had walked three days a week for a year: The brain scans revealed that the size of the hippocampus grew by around 2 percent in the walking group—a large increase that reversed the age-related decline by one to two years.

Active and consistent walking has also demonstrated gains in recall tests as it allows us to retain and retrieve more memories of our daily interactions that have been enhanced by physical activity and increased levels of protein in the brain responsible for learning.

Gratitude Journaling

Frequent journaling has a huge range of health and well-being benefits, including:

- Enhancing your self-awareness and self-consciousness
- Increasing your self-compassion, which allows you to better appreciate others
- Providing opportunities for reflection to strengthen and improve your conversations and relationships with your family, friends, students, and team members
- Giving you a chance to remember the fun you had throughout your day
- Providing context as it helps you to respond, not react

- Encouraging a deeper level of empathy-based listening and learning

I begin every day with a moment of gratitude, with active reflection on what I am grateful for, which helps with my work-family-life balance. Every morning, this gives me time to quiet my brain and focus on my learning before I launch my busy day, which is consumed with a list of work products to create, emails to answer, and video webinars to plan and present.

I also close each day with a moment of thanks. This helps me to have closure for the day, focus on what I accomplished, note where I might have gotten off track, and consider what actions I will need to take tomorrow to resolve the challenges I faced. Closure is so important to me emotionally; otherwise, it's hard for me to relax and shut down the to-do list in my head.

ARE YOU LOOKING FOR MORE WAYS TO EXPRESS YOUR GRATITUDE?
Here is a collection of 10-Minute Gratitude Journals to assist your efforts. Feel free to download, print, and share with others to spread the gift of gratitude.

Watching Ted Talks

Many days, I watch a Ted Talk for an extra dose of inspiration, a brain-based learning experience, or science exploration. My creative mind yearns for learning in a stimulating video with a creative plot. I love learning, and when I can discover a new teaching practice to promote existing study, a self-improvement or leadership strategy methodology, or a video to make me laugh, it's fun and rewarding. It also makes my mind ready for the day with fresh creative energy.

TEDTALK
Here is a TedTalk video as an example to really make you think and see how you can modify your actions to influence others—even as a very young child. "How every child can thrive by age five."

Enjoying Essential Oils

I have recently discovered the healing, calming effects of essential oils. Recent research conducted at the Mayo Clinic used essential oil aromatherapy as a remedy for pain management in people with severe pain, anxiety, and nausea, and for helping people to deal with life-changing events such as cancer, traumatic brain injuries, and stroke.

Is our nose a pathway to our big beautiful brains?

Through a friend, I met Jamie Peterson, a wellness advocate and doTERRA essential oils consultant. I talked with Jamie about the potential for essential oils to help my son's pain and my own menopausal symptoms. We bonded immediately over our love of chemistry, and I shared that I received the Chemistry of the Year award from Western Technical College in La Crosse, Wisconsin, back in 1994.

Jamie explained that essential oils can aid in relaxation to help with anxiety, regulate pain, and help people feel more in control of their emotional state. She sent me a sample packet of essential oils to try, a blend called Adaptiv Peppermint, and Balance, which she thought would help both my son and I.

I was elated to find that within the first few days of trying the essential oils, it gave me some relief of my hot flashes and a sense of calming and grounding to help me focus during my most stressful days. My son found that the Deep Blue lotion with peppermint essential oil aided in the relief of his achy arthritic joints and bones. Since then, I've incorporated using essential oils into my daily habits.

Cooking

Another daily habit I've fostered is preparing and eating nutritious food. This is a top priority for me, for my social and mental well-being, and because my family has a long history of heart disease and cancer. For this reason, I buy organic food when I can and prepare and eat healthy meals. I enjoy small quantities of dark chocolate and sweet snacks at times, but I eat them only in very small amounts to experience a quick taste, enough to make me smile.

I love to cook, bake, and come up with my own special culinary combinations and master new gourmet recipes, so that I can pass them on to my own children and grandchildren. This culinary heritage and influence came from my grandmother Iola. As a role model and culinary mentor to me, she taught me that one must believe in oneself and nurture one's interests in learning to truly be happy! Using my imagination and talents in cooking has been a meaningful lifetime experience, as it serves as a stress outlet by giving me a better work-life balance and an opportunity to highlight my beautiful creations. Most of the time, these gourmet meals and decadent sweets are a win for my friends and family to enjoy. My closest friends and family members urge me to write my own cookbook, so that could be a possible follow-up to my women-in-leadership book series.

I've shared my leadership habits and rituals. What are yours?

Our everyday rituals, routines, and customs are different and satisfying for each and every one of us. How we find and make time for significant and purposeful events in our lives is a product of our determined thoughts. It is also up to us to give priority to the most important and positive things in our lives that concern us to bring about progress. It is up to each of us to take responsibility and follow through with these required steps of action, to mold these life-changing behaviors that will have an effect on our futures and eventually imagine and reflect our best selves every day.

> *We are what we repeatedly do. Excellence, then, is not an act, but a habit.*
>
> —Aristotle

MODELING EMPATHY, INTUITION, AND COLLABORATION

Compelling neuroscience research teaches us that women's brains are wired for empathy, intuition, and collaboration—traits that people are looking for in their leaders today. Women leaders have identified relationship building as a vital indicator and a central element in building successful leadership teams.

If coordination and teamwork break down among team members, the whole team will struggle. This is a direct reflection of your leadership model. That's why you need to recognize your leadership qualities and tactics to develop your team with sympathy, intuition, and teamwork as the foundation of your company or association. Allow yourself time to earn a buy-in from your peers and the leadership team and to build confidence, working relationships, and a professional partnership with each person on the team. Your professional character and reputation are dependent on your track record in leadership. Ask yourself, *How can I concentrate on and prioritize developing relationships and model empathy, intuition, and teamwork?*

It is important to use research-based team-building activities to foster and model positive teamwork methods. These are called Total Participation Techniques (TPT). They are opportunities to build community-based relationships among colleagues, busiess leaders, and K-12 educators. For example, some of these activities include the following.

- **Inclusive openings and optimistic closings:** This is a personalized technique in which everyone has a voice to share an understanding or reflection based on a prompt. This technique reveals each participant's prior knowledge on the subject, so everyone can empathize and better understand the perspectives and viewpoints shared by others. Sometimes they are silly, fun prompts, such as "What one word will guide your innovators' compass, help you make quality decisions, pursue your goals, and become the best human possible?" Other times they are an everyday scenario like "What happened today to make you smile?" These encourage sharing and lighten the feel of the room. Many people can relate to the information that has been shared.
- **Think pair shares:** People are given a prompt, question, or scenario to ponder. Then they are paired, and each person shares their un-

Visit this site to learn more about SEL and gratitude inclusive openings and optimistic closings.

derstanding, and viewpoints with their partner. They gain the other person's perspective. Then the entire group assembles, and each pair shares their findings. The larger group documents the findings and looks for trends.

I have collaborated with many educational and corporate teams around the world. Leaders everywhere are talking about the value of partnerships and collaboration. But many companies and organizations have never really shaped or showcased what a successful team does differently to make them highly collaborative and communicative. What does a product management team look and sound like?

This is where a successful servant leadership style comes into play. You develop your leadership base by engaging in human relationships first. Then they are modeled and facilitated with the professional learning community—the closest individuals you work with on a daily basis, such as your staff and colleagues.

As discussed in chapter 3, servant leadership is a philosophy and a collection of practices that enrich the lives of people, develop stronger institutions, and eventually create a fair, equitable, more compassionate environment. Servant leaders put the desires and needs of their followers ahead of their own interests and needs. These leaders put a high priority on the growth of their teams, striving to create a society where team members share influence. Servant leadership starts with the innate feeling that one needs to serve first. Then aspiring to lead is a deliberate decision.

Dr. Dirk van Dierendonck, professor of human resource management at the Rotterdam School of Management, Erasmus University, Netherlands, researched leadership and found the best leaders have the following qualities:

- **Empowering and improving people:** This is about empowering everybody to take responsibility for their own decisions. The chief respects the strengths and skills of those she/he leads and invites them to run alongside her/him. The idea is to promote the personal development of everyone on the team.

- **Humility:** With this simple mentality, the chief understands that she/he does not know everything, and the workers have important skills and expertise to offer. Data reveals that modesty predicts good leadership, according to Dr. Robert Hogan, founder and president of Hogan Assessments. Humility includes mitigating gaps in rank, listening to colleagues, seeking advice, accepting errors, and being able to change direction when a strategy appears unsuccessful.
- **Authenticity:** People value authenticity and instinctively condemn fraudulent conduct. A leader can be seen as authentic if she/he behaves with dignity, meets up on undertakings, and demonstrates maturity in her/his actions. The leader must prove that she is true to herself and must inspire her supporters to be true to themselves as well.
- **Interpersonal acceptance:** A great leader has the capacity to understand people and, listen to their emotions, and learn what motivates them. There is also a leadership tradition in which compassion and grace are taught because it is recognized that people will and do make mistakes. By welcoming everyone at school, from the janitor to every teacher and student with their specific viewpoints, the leader makes each person understand that they matter.
- **Providing guidance:** This is what leadership is all about—providing direction. All should know what is required of them, and what their specific objectives are. Ideally, the servant leader will excel in building an atmosphere where engagement is seen as meaningful. Dr. Dierendonck explains, "In order to have guidance, the servant leader must make work interactive and adapt it to the strengths and needs of workers."
- **Stewardship:** Dr. Dierendonck sees stewardship as a desire to take responsibility for a greater organization and to rely on contribution rather than power and self-interest. The servant leader sets a precedent for people to emulate, modeling how to behave in the collective interest.

My observations of and experiences with the leadership role while an undergraduate at Viterbo University provided me with a learning opportunity to experience and place the role model of leadership in motion as an instructor and as the CEO of my women-in-leadership business. The liberal arts curriculum and fundamental principles at Viterbo University trained my teaching stewardship and corporate leadership paths in the following ways.

- Relevant, purposeful, compassionate educational methods
- Empathy-based humanitarian listening and speech skills
- Dynamic facilitation and training of instructional methods to meet all learners
- Importance of links to hands-on learning bibliography
- Ethical servant leadership to model and change for others

This teaching and servant leadership pathway shaped and continues to transform my technical teaching and learning presence. It is a direct reflection of the excellent education I have received, the relationships and advice of Viterbo's professors and support staff, and the strength of the message of service and ethical leadership that I value in everything I do. Thanks to it, I have had a positive effect on many students and educational leaders in our great, beautiful country over the past 25 years. I am so grateful to have had the chance to receive my college education and degree from Viterbo University.

Apparently Viterbo University is very proud of my servant leadership work in the field as well, as most recently I have received the 2020 Distinguished Alumni Award from the College of Education, Engineering, Letters and Sciences as Professional Achievement. And this past spring of 2021, I received Entrepreneur of the Year award from Viterbo University. This most recent award was based on how my women-in-leadership company is changing the face of education and has revolutionized K-12 teaching and learning strategies and leadership approaches during the time of the pandemic. Yet most importantly, my futuristic vision was honored of how to reinvent and transform education, to meet the needs of today's diverse students with culturally relevant, empathy filled practices, and how to truly engage our Millennial and Gen Z educators. I am forever grateful for both of these honors and for the knowledge that my collaborative team is making an educational difference in the lives of our future generations of learners and educators!

I'm very much a visual learner and thinker. I need images and icons to guide my big-picture thinking to follow through with my leadership tasks.

DESIGNING YOUR LIFE

LOVE- PLAY-WORK-HEALTH BALANCE WORKSHEET

- Mark your dashboard as it currently exists
- What do you observe?

- If you could make one incremental adjustment, what would it be? Redraw your improved dashboard.
- What would you get if you could attain this revised level of balance? How would life (really) change for you?

CURRENT

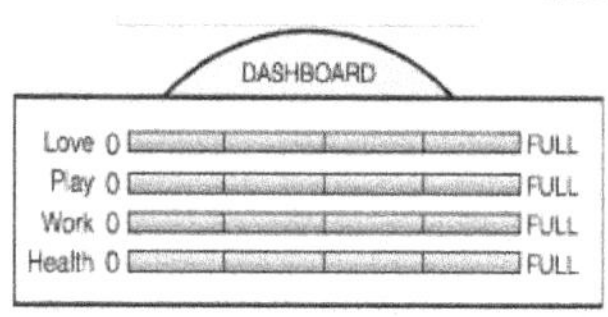

REVISED

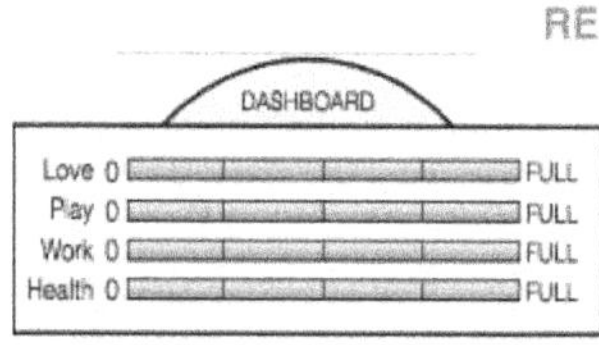

- What incremental change could you attempt to move in this direction? What would it take for you to live this way for two weeks?

Yet some days are filled with so many tasks to do, it can feel very daunting. That's when I use the 80/20 rule, which is also known as the Pareto Principle. It can extend to so many aspects of our personal and professional lives. The Pareto Principle notes that 80 percent of the results come from 20 percent of the inputs.

The question remains: How can we give priority to work-life-balance when something feels so important? For me, this principle is helpful when deciding what needs my overall attention. I apply this maxim to enterprise and marketing when determining where to invest my energy and money.

The greatest hurdle to optimizing this time is failing to create a schedule and adhere to it. By taking the time to build a weekly routine and a work list, you will no longer experience the constant burden of knowing something is a priority that stimulates your stress hormones and triggers your fight-or-flight response. Adding this tension to your workday is unnecessary. Each of us has enough stress without having to add to it!

Let's calculate how much the effective 20 percent of your workday is and build a roadmap for how to find this time and what to do with it. Of course, you're going to need to squeeze in other duties, but they're supposed to be things that don't consume all of your brain capacity or time. The most critical 20 percent is relegated to those sections of time that are most valuable to you, to your deliberate relationship building, and to the application of your servant leadership style.

I was immediately fascinated when I stumbled across the Love-Play-Dashboard in the book *Designing Your Life*. It's a tool for calculating the fullness (and balance) of your life.

To use this tool, you assess your current love, play, work, and health. For each, ask yourself if that area of your life is completely full, three-quarters full, half full, or empty. Mark that on the "current dashboard" below. Then consider: If you could adjust your love, play, work, and health by making small changes, what would it look like? Mark that on the "revised dashboard" below. Ask yourself the questions below.

Play is the highest level of research.
—Albert Einstein

Here's how to assess the four categories on the dashboard.

- **Love:** A love dashboard is a test of the quality of your interactions and social stability. Think about your place in your family and in society at large. Do you have enough time for your partner, children, relatives, friends, acquaintances, and others in your social network? What relationships could you instantly improve with a quick email, call, or Zoom?
- **Play:** The play dashboard is the indicator of pleasure in your life. This covers things that you do solely for fun, not related to reward or competition. They could include sports, arts, and relaxation such as people-watching in a park. This category is most frequently neglected. Some people don't prioritize it. Other people see it as a waste of time. But play may be the most important thing, giving us a sense of completeness, pleasure, and well-being. If you would like to learn more about the value of play, I highly recommend that you check out the LEGO Education and Social Emotional Development Global Research Report on our big beautiful brains. It inspires and develops our life-learning confidence and curious minds through tangible hands-on learning discovery experiences.
- **Work:** The work dashboard covers everything you do in your workday. This may be paid jobs, as well as voluntary labor, homemaking, and childcare. Jobs bring us a sense of identity and are important to our self-esteem. How will you score your commitment, satisfaction, and the value of your work?
- **Health:** Your health gauge should encompass your physical, emotional, and mental health. Of course, it's important to exercise and eat healthy foods, but it's also important to take care of your mental well-being. Do you feel happy and optimistic on most days, or do you feel stressed or burned out? Is one part of your well-being suffering while another is thriving?

Putting Purpose into Practice

ADOPT NEW LIFE HABITS

Let's explore and discover my favorite habits to extend your transformational leadership approach and add to your toolkit of leadership best practices.

10-Minute Journals

Can you find just 10 minutes each day to journal? Try to find a consistent, best time for you. It might be in the morning, over lunch, after work, or before bed.

You could buy a journal or a blank book. You could journal on a Note-taking app on your phone or laptop.

Ted Talk Videos

Each day, can you take a break to watch a Ted Talk? They are usually only a few minutes long. Find Ted Talks that resonate with your personal and professional desires to help you on your leadership path. Visit *www.ted.com/talk.* If you subscribe to the Ted Talk channel, they email a new video each day to inspire you to start your day well.

FREE JOURNAL PAGES

Rather than buying a journal, you could download journal pages, such as from this site.

FINDING BALANCE AND PURPOSE IN YOUR LIFE SLIDE DECK

If you are looking for more meaningful work-life-family balance in your life, please check out my entire slide deck on "Finding Balance and Purpose in Your Life" to gain new critical insights on how to make leadership experience transformational and how to visualize your best self each and every day.

Chapter 5

GROW YOUR LEADERSHIP CONFIDENCE

Increase Your Cognitive Presence and Positive Genius Influence

CONNECTING THE LEARNING DOTS WITH AN EDUCATIONAL LEADERSHIP INFLUENCE

Have you ever been told that you ask too many questions or talk too much?

Since I was a very young girl, I have asked a lot of questions, trying to understand the world around me. I was "one of those students'" who many teachers would roll their eyes at any time I lifted my hand, blurted out the answer, fidgeted, tapped my foot uncontrollably, or disrupted to share my point of view or ask a question. I had to ask a lot of questions and then follow up with even more clarifying questions to apply my current interpretation. Once I had a clearer understanding of the concept, I often had to take my new learning on a test drive to prove to myself and others that I could master it.

My persistent questioning got the best of me sometimes. Still to this day, it can trip me up—for better or for worse. Yet looking back at my childhood, it wasn't an option for me to fail, and I had to ask a lot of questions to succeed.

My research-driven thinking complemented my need for hands-on learning and helped me to link the learning dots to my physical environment. When one of these two learning attributes was out of sync, I struggled to understand why. I got nervous, felt unruly, and could not pay attention because my focus was lacking.

As a child, I did not have the capacity to self-regulate my acts and be self-aware of my behavior. I wish the Social Emotional Learning (SEL) curriculum would have been offered during my high school years. Today, it is. There are several SEL curriculums, and the gold standard is CASEL. They set our standards to support emotional learning. They are instructional approaches to help build a stronger community of learning. They help students empathize, understand others with special needs, and support each other. They are also used in schools to help teachers proactively handle mental health situations. After the COVID-19 pandemic, SEL has exploded in K-12. In order for students to be successful, they need to feel safe. The SEL strategies are essential to support that.

When I was a child, a lot of people complained about my behavior, verbal outbursts, and fidgeting. They constantly advised me to be more self-aware about my actions. Instead I wish they had given me the opportunity to learn through examples of how I should be involved and how to better regulate my off-task behaviors.

Looking back now, I understand that all of those constructive criticisms, negative experiences, and verbal reinforcements by adults and my peers created life-long neuronal impressions inside my brain. These neuronal learning pathways directed my critical thought process and decision-making skills.

As an adult, I have been able to develop self-awareness of my decisions to fully concentrate on what is most important to grow my career and care for my family. It wasn't an easy process to get to this point. I eventually got here because influential women role models provided me with time to ask questions, listened to consider my viewpoint, and provided me with hands-on learning experiences to discover, explore, and fulfill my passions.

Do you remember thinking about your career aspirations, ambitions, and even fears as an elementary or middle schooler? Were your dreams inspired by an older sister, grandmother, or another woman in your life? Were your dreams linked to an encounter that resonated with you motivating you to believe that you might contribute to something better in our world?

If so, I bet you remember these memories as if they happened yesterday. Yet for some, like me, those events happened many years ago. It's been almost five decades since I connected the learning dots about how and why I've landed in my STEM leadership profession where I'm in my life today.

What's the time frame for you? Do you remember the crucial learning moments in your life when caring people inspired your career ambitions and encouraged you to fulfill your learning passions?

One of my pivotal learning moments happened in Mrs. Becker's 3rd/4th grade class in northeast Iowa. She was a kind, loving educator who recognized the value of personalized learning and differentiated instruction to fulfill the learning needs of every child in her classroom. I was a very busy, active, strong-willed young girl. My attention span was equal to that of goldfish swimming back and forth in a goldfish bowl—about five seconds.

Mrs. Becker found out early on how to use my busy energy for the good of my education. She often chose me to help troubleshoot and figure out solutions to problems in our elementary classroom. She assigned me to set up and run the film strip projector for our class, to set up hands-on learning manipulatives at student-centered rotating stations, and to coach other students to set up scientific, literacy, and math hands-on learning activities.

My life was forever changed by this caring teacher who did not know at the time that she was wearing the hat of a career and life coach. These experiences helped me to feel comfortable, gave me the opportunity to take safe risks, allowed me to ask a lot of questions, and enabled me to develop trust through learning by play, tinkering, and creation experiences. These opportunities encouraged me to share my voice, visual thinking, struggles with learning, and new experience as a peer mentor with my classmates while developing resiliency.

From this story, you can glean the best practice teaching and learning techniques. If I hadn't had Mrs. Becker as a powerful, caring educator in my life, my learning journey would have been far different than what it is today. Most certainly, I would have lost my passion in STEM and opted for a career that wasn't as rewarding.

Women role models can really make a difference in the careers of girls and young adults. They can help you to connect the learning dots in your own life. This means that I can identify my women-in-leadership passion and knowing I want to help improve another girl's life to help her find her own success and find something that truly interests her. Doing this helps you develop your leadership confidence. The more you model and grow your own leadership, the more you can influence others so girls can see other women leading. Knowing you are a part of someone else's life builds your leadership confidence.

As you connect the learning dots in your education and career and look for opportunities to help younger women leaders do the same, ask yourself the following questions. Then consider asking these questions of a young woman leader you mentor.

- What are you most interested in learning about and why?
- How, why, and where do you learn best?
- What do you love to do that your teacher or leader might not know about?
- How do you like to learn and work with your classmates or colleagues?
- What does learning success look like to you?
- How does your work make you feel?
- What types of learning experiences come easy to you and why?
- Would you peer coach a classmate or a colleague with a leadership activity?

The following resources will jump start your student advocacy with the support of your women-in-leadership presence.

- Advisor, Teacher, and Role Models
- Becoming Visible: STEM Role Models For Mentoring Disabled Students

THE VALUE OF STEM

By the end of middle school years, many girls lose interest in STEM-focused experiences and careers. This occurs because of the following evidence-based criteria.

- Currently many schools and business offices undervalue women's points of view.
- Girls lack access to realistic STEM learning experience and equal access to STEM materials and resources, compared with boys. For example, the after-school coding clubs and robotics clubs were originally only offered to boys—girls were excluded. Along the same lines, some sports activities still exclude girls.
- Negative myths abound about girls interested in STEM being perceived as "geeks and nerds."
- If girls don't have the access to STEM, they then don't get the STEM growth mindset, which is an individual's capacity to learn STEM and at the same time build content knowledge around concepts and have the opportunity to seek and find their STEM learning passion. If a girl doesn't get experience in STEM, she doesn't know what she doesn't know, and she might settle for something less.
- Because there are fewer women STEM teachers, girls today still lack STEM modeling by female educators and caregivers.
- A lack of ethnic women role models and mentors in the STEM and computer science workforce results in girls and young women not envisioning their future selves in STEM.

Educational leaders must afford all girls and young women with more opportunities to experience STEM as a compassionate "lean-in'" culture of practice. STEM activities should involve all of our students, and STEM activities must be prioritized in learner-centered and invention literacy–focused classrooms.

Educators need to break the STEM stereotypes and identify, recognize, and change their own unconscious bias they may have with girls in STEM.

Educators need to start this task very early in a young girl's education. We all need to reach, connect with, and mentor girls in their early childhood years. We need to provide our students access to women STEM mentors, women role models, and women inspired activities to ensure all girls and young women can dream about and be active creators of their futures.

The caring, influential educator Mrs. Becker, my 3rd/4th grade teacher who encouraged me scholastically and emotionally throughout my grade school years, guided me with subtle and motivational instructional methods and insights that uncovered my STEM learning passions and women-in-leadership career goals. Her empathic teaching and learning methods contributed to my educational leadership career as a women-in-leadership strategist, educational mentor, and STEM innovation specialist.

I made a life-long vow to transform the leadership of STEM in education and technology companies for all women. I will continue to fight the good fight, to model what is right for both girls and boys. I will continue to coach, inspire, and shape the next generation of girls and young women students through a caring, lean-in culture.

- Challenging Our Gendered Idea Of Mentorship
- Her-Story Global Collaboration Project To Be The Role Models for All Girls
- Role Models and Mentors
- Role Model Strategies
- SciGirls Role Model Profiles
- CareerGirls
- STEAM Careers For The 21st Century
- The Roles Woman Can Play as Leadership Mentors
- Why Girls Need More Mentors in STEM

CREATING A CULTURE OF FEEDBACK FOR SUCCESSFUL COMMUNICATION AND COLLABORATION

Feedback is imperative to grow and nurture your leadership confidence. Without feedback, we don't know what we need to change or adjust. It provides us a quick evaluation and assessment of the how/why we're doing so we can modify our practice to improve our leadership style.

Feedback is an important part of all relationships both professional and personal. We are always listening for verbal feedback and watching for nonverbal clues as well. That's why a culture of feedback is important for successful communication and collaboration.

Creating a safe, conducive work environment is vital to establishing a responsive culture of feedback among colleagues and employees. This is one of the most important elements for the effectiveness of every team. In this work culture, everyone's voices are heard, and everyone engages in constructive listening and seeking to learn. Everyone's feedback is listened to and valued.

According to experts at Cambridge University, feedback can be the most valuable asset to any organization. Bob Dignen, the author of a Cambridge University blog, identifies the following five reasons why feedback is significant.

1. **Feedback is there all the time—every time we talk or listen to another person.** It's the sound of our voices, the words we choose, and the awkward, quiet pauses that we allow. We express feedback all of the time, even nonverbally, offering clues to how much we trust, admire, enjoy, like, or even hate the person in front of us.
2. **Feedback is just another term for good listening.** When one person responds to another, she wants to experience two very fundamental things. First, she wants to know that she's been heard. Second, she wants to believe that what she said has some kind of meaning. If the speaker doesn't get one or both of these things, she can easily become confused or even annoyed.
3. **Feedback is an opportunity to motivate.** Positive feedback is another word for encouragement. It is all about taking the opportunity to show gratitude for a job well done, in the hope of motivating a person to do even more jobs even better. Few corporate leaders, school administrators, and even peers have time to praise others for something well achieved. This causes them to lose the opportunity to inspire positive emotions and dedication in their team members who are doing well.
4. **Feedback is important for performance development.** For many people, feedback feels like a critique or attack. However, feedback should be neither of those. It is a positive gesture designed to deal with under-performance in a proactive manner and to improve performance to a higher level.

5. **Feedback is a means to keep learning.** Receiving feedback and learning from it is the best way to stop repeating mistakes, hear how people encounter working with you, and strengthen your leadership methods.

However, feedback is only valid and helpful if you interpret the feedback, create an action plan to make changes, assess the actions you took to record the improvement or to recognize another setback if it occurs, and then begin a feedback loop with your supervisor or peers to enhance the feedback and results-driven process. Good leadership takes a lot of work!

There may be times when you don't get the feedback that you need. This is where the art of "reading the room" is key to the success of the leadership model. If your supervisor or peers aren't giving you feedback, read their body language to receive some feedback indirectly.

Someone who exhibits one or more of the following behaviors is likely to be disengaged, uninterested, or dissatisfied.

- Folded arms in front of the body
- Facial expressions that are minimal or tight
- The body shifted away from you
- Downcast eyes, making minimal eye contact

These pointers will assist you in adjusting your body language so that you make a good first impression.

- Maintain an open stance. Be at ease, but don't slouch! Place your hands by your sides and sit or stand straight. Standing with your hands on your hips might convey aggressiveness.
- Use a strong handshake. But don't get too far ahead of yourself! You don't want the other person to feel awkward, aggressive, or uncomfortable.
- Maintain constant eye contact. Try to keep the other person's focus on you for a few seconds at a time. This will demonstrate to them that you are honest and committed.
- Keep your hands away from your face. If you do this when answering questions, it may be interpreted as dishonesty. While this isn't always the

case, you should avoid messing with your hair or scratching your nose in order to project trustworthiness.

You probably won't be surprised to read that men and women both give and respond differently to feedback. In my Executive Women in Leadership course at Cornell University, Professor Deborah Streeter discussed the gender aspects of both giving and receiving feedback. These learning examples provide me with visionary practices to model and incorporate in my discussions and everyday encounters with all genders.

Most supervisors are unwilling to offer both men and women difficult and constructive feedback. However, a women-in-the-workplace survey showed that women receive feedback significantly less often than their male colleagues.

More than 20 percent of women are less likely than males to obtain complex feedback to enhance performance. Furthermore, supervisors are more likely to hesitate to give feedback to women because of the fear of unpleasant results. This is less important if male employees are to get input.

The feedback women do receive is frequently imprecise and non-specific.

Stanford University academics Shelley Correll and Caroline Simard examined a variety of performance assessments in a Harvard Business Review article. They wanted to know why women were having difficulty progressing in their jobs.

According to the paper, "Our research reveals that women are systematically less likely to get explicit feedback related to outcomes, both when they receive praise and when the feedback is developmental."

A sample of performance evaluations revealed that women consistently received less constructive comments than males. When women did receive comments to help them grow, Correll and Simard discovered that it was frequently centered on their communication style. They point out that, despite the fact that communication is an important skill for employee growth, women frequently receive negative criticism about their communication style.

The Executive Women in Leadership course also outlined specific case studies and learning scenarios, which helped me to build my leadership confidence and to improve my communication and constructive leadership conversations with both genders—without feeling threatened or territorial.

There is an art to giving and receiving feedback. If feedback is not handled correctly, it will have a detrimental effect on the confidence and community of your colleagues. I know this from personal experience.

I once worked in a toxic environment that was completely bereft of helpful feedback—a K-12 service agency in western Wisconsin. At that job, one administrator modeled very weak leadership, loved to micromanage, and stifled women in leadership roles. The only feedback he ever gave was unhelpful. It did not address the purpose of the learning outcome, nor did it encourage or coach an individual to strive for improvement. It appeared the feedback was more one sided and would only benefit him, instead of focusing on growing the organization and building stronger working relationships among my colleagues.

To compound the problem, the organization projected a top-down management style. This administrator tried his hardest to impede our women's creative and collaborative thinktanks. Sometimes, he firmly pulled the reins back on women who were making revolutionary strides and progress in teaching and learning.

The lesson I learned from working with this administrator was: If something doesn't sound or look right, listen to your gut. Try your best but know in the end, it might not work out well.

I tried to cope with this incompetent leader for almost a year. Ironically, this was one of the best educational experiences of my life. Why? Because it showed me what not to do as a leader. I saw firsthand how leadership—good or bad—affects so many people in so many ways. I learned how important it is to both give and receive helpful feedback. And this experience prompted me to leave the organization and start my own company!

While working in this organization, I first discovered my passion for guiding and promoting professional learning activities for K-12 educators. Although I did work with this one challenging administrator, at the same time I was strongly encouraged by my first woman mentor, Myrna Daugherty, who I mentioned earlier, and a team of compassionate women leaders—including tech director Jan Wee, curriculum and tech specialist Jodie Hoscheit, and distance learning director, Carol Popelka.

This team of amazing, talented women, so gifted in their areas of expertise, took the time to get to know me both professionally and personally. They listened to my questions and provided me with authentic, helpful feedback. They mentored me to hone my speaking, writing, and facilitating skills. They pushed me to my limits at times when I need to be pushed, such as when I questioned my writing skills when applying for six-figure instructional technology grants to help fund technology and learning resources for 26 school districts!

These creative women colleagues also knew how to celebrate a job well done. We made time to pause and enjoy the moment when we landed those six-figure grants and when we developed and delivered new tech integration programs. Those celebrations brought us stronger together, helping us to realize we are more alike than we are different.

These women supported me during the challenging times with this administrator who tried to stifle my forward-thinking leadership vision as I tried to develop creative vocational and STEM projects. Within seven years, I developed very strong personal and professional relationships with these strong, brave women leaders as they nurtured my confidence, resiliency, dignity, pride, and perseverance to sustain my innovative vision of my best leadership self. These were some of my very first mentors in technology leadership. They trusted in me and helped me realize my vision for my women-in-leadership company!

I personally take pride in my ability to give helpful feedback to other people. By giving feedback, I have a lasting effect on the lives of the people I meet and work with. The greatest gift I can give them is helping them to develop their own positive genius. This gift gives rise to positivity and pleasure in one's life and affects and resonates with others. My positive genius has allowed me to create a message of good for others, as I share my stories of hope, happiness, and even failures.

The challenging times at that K-12 service agency changed my thinking and inspired me to pursue a women's leadership paradigm that provides a vision for what servant leadership should look and feel like for everyone, including the value of quality feedback. As I formed these philosophies, I realized enough was enough, and I began thinking that I needed to make a career change.

But then, opportunity knocked. I was invited to be a keynote speaker at the SchoolNet International Conference in South Africa. The toxic administrator refused my request to attend and speak. I tried to explain to him why this opportunity was so valuable to me as an educator and director of education technology. The administrator couldn't see past his own ego to understand the importance of this global professional event—both to me and to the organization. I believe he didn't want to admit how the opportunity would catapult my career to the next level. But he also couldn't see how much this opportunity could positively affect our organization, too.

That's when I realized that he was not actively listening. Nor was he taking any of my feedback into consideration. It was apparent that his head was very far up his own ass. I wondered, *Why would he do this?* I felt that he had to be in control, and in order to do that, he had to hold me back.

The feeling of being controlled by a dominant male flooded my brain with memories of my first marriage. I was only 18 years old, parent to a two-year-old, and had been married to the man who got me pregnant as a teenager. My then-husband was verbally and physically abusive. He was controlling in his male dominance. Using "Catholic guilt," my mother had forced me to marry this man I did not love. I think that my mom believed that his abusive, controlling demeanor would disappear once we got married. She was wrong.

I filed for divorce within two and a half years. But during those two and a half years, I incurred horrible verbal abuse from my then-husband and also from some of his family. I also sustained a broken arm, a broken nose, and two cracked ribs. Another child was conceived—without my consent.

By observing his family, I saw a generational pattern of long-term abuse. I had to escape with my children to break free from this abusive environment. I knew if we did not, we would not survive.

My abusive first marriage made me acutely sensitive to controlling, male dominance tactics, such as a male forcing his viewpoints upon me. At the first hint of this behavior, my defenses kick in and sound "be aware" alarms in my head and gut.

When the toxic administrator denied my request to speak at the South African event, squelching it as he had so many opportunities before, I thought, *This is the last time he will do this to me.* I knew in my heart that the speaking engagement opportunity was the sign of a lifetime. It was the impetus to get me out of the current terrible situation I was in with a non-supportive, verbally abusive administrator.

In a meeting with him, my heightened anxiety combined with feelings from my prior years of verbal and physical abuse. I blurted out, "How far is your head up your own ass that you cannot see the learning potential here?"

Yes, I said it! And I could not take it back.

It did not go over very well.

In hindsight, I should have "read the room" better because the administrator displayed clear signs of his displeasure. Without giving me helpful verbal feedback, his body was giving me plenty of nonverbal feedback. His tone was rigid and harsh, and his face was so red that he resembled a red-hot tamale! I thought he was going to explode!

He wanted to fire me for insubordination.

But I didn't give him the satisfaction. Instead, I quit.

It was time for me to venture out on my own. I was ready to lead with intentional purpose and integrity. I couldn't wait to model how a woman could successfully lead with servant leadership.

The icing on the cake was I did deliver that educational technology keynote speech in South Africa in 2009. It was one of the most inspiring keynotes of my lifetime! I'm humbled to say that I was invited back in 2011 and 2013 to continue to inspire and collaborate with South African educational leaders.

Hopefully this story has illustrated the power of helpful feedback by giving an example of non-helpful feedback. But it's important to acknowledge that not all men have such short-sighted, narrow-minded visions of women in leadership. I believe it's a minority of male administrators who lack first-hand learning experiences of awareness to appreciate the gifts that women leaders bring to a company. These men lack awareness of what an effective leadership paradigm might look, sound, and feel like to revitalize and invest in their employees through a shared working community led by an effective servant leader. These antiquated male leaders have a very difficult time admitting what they don't know. Their own egos, arrogance, and selfishness trip up their thinking and actions.

That being said, I also have worked with and been inspired by many male influencers. Jack Hemesath, my father, was one of my biggest advocates. He supported my decision to leave the K-12 service agency. The conversations I had with my ailing father in 2008 motivated me to start my own business. When I visited him, he would tell me that I wasn't my usual bubbly, energetic self. He knew that something was bothering me.

This led to deep conversations about how unhappy I was working for the K-12 service agency, especially working with the toxic administrator. Together, my dad and I talked through my options, which we distilled down to starting my own EdTech company or a catering business. I had always been inspired by my, grandma Iola, who owned her own catering business, and two of my passions have always been cooking and baking.

Now you may be asking, how did you decide to choose the EdTech company focusing over a catering company? Well, it all has to do with relationships, and my clientele base was primarily made up of K-12 administrative leaders, educators, and business leaders. I knew these connections would provide me with an already established clientele base. My existing K-12 and highered clients already knew of my professional character, work ethic, quality of work, and my organized and timely deliverables. By the time the word got out that I left the K-12 organizations and started my own EdTech company, the phone was ringing off the hook, and my email was overflowing with professional learning workshops and presentation requests. So I knew in my heart and my pocketbook that I made the right decision, even though the catering and bakery business still may be part of my next adventure as a future career possibility.

Backed by my father's emotional encouragement and in his spirit, I ventured on my own, setting up Innovative Educator Consulting Corporation in the winter of 2009. It was the greatest decision of my life. It has been the most challenging and satisfying work of my career—so far.

Fast forward 13 years: My company has expanded into a global EdTech leadership corporation, representing a team of innovative, talented women master educators from around the country. Each day, these women inspire me by their innovative thinking and creative mindsets. They also provide me feedback and advice as we expand the creative leadership services of the corporation.

Over the years, I have discovered that teams receiving daily input in a constructive, nurturing manner will aspire to continue to do better for the company. When they see their leader trusts them, both personally and professionally, they feel appreciated. In turn, when a person feels appreciated, she will perform at a higher level, strive to increase her talents, work to attain greatness, and realize that she will receive the gift of respect from her leader. Positive, consistent, timely feedback is the key to success. An affirmation of thanks for a job well done leads to the growth of the company. All members of a team are honored when leaders create a community of appreciative, innovative thinkers and doers.

Today, I show my appreciation to my creative team of EdTech consultants by celebrating often. I made a point to continue this even with the COVID-19 pandemic, despite great physical distance between our working-from-home locations. #TogetherWeAreBetter.

Putting Purpose into Practice

DEVELOP YOUR LEADERSHIP PRESENCE

As you have learned from my previous chapters, our big beautiful brains constantly evolve in response to new learning leadership opportunities you participate in. You are in control of which brain circuits you activate. Each time you learn something new and put it into practice, you develop your leadership presence. This will give you a joyful sense of hope as you develop confidence in your leadership style. You will resonate a new cognitive presence and positive genius with your team. Practice makes permanent, so let's step up your game and strengthen your leadership presence.

The following three questioning techniques will help you to develop your leadership presence—by increasing the trust with your colleagues. These techniques will improve the way you ask clarifying questions to understand and to have more meaningful conversations.

These techniques also demonstrate how you "lean-in" by asking probing questions and by modeling intentionality. You'll show your interest in your colleagues and in their leadership styles.

Choose one question from each category below. Set a goal to pose those three questions at work or even at home to have more meaningful, purposeful conversations and invest in the people you are conversing with.

Questions to Establish Collegial Relationships and Trust

- So...(then restate)
- In other words...
- What I'm hearing is...
- From what I hear you say...
- I'm hearing a few things...
- As I listen to you, I'm realizing that...
- Please explain that another way...

Clarifying Questions to Activate Meaningful Conversations and Listen with Empathy

- Please tell me a little more about...
- Let me make sure I understand...
- I'm interested in hearing more about...
- Please give me an example, so I can be sure I understand...
- Are you suggesting that...
- Tell me what you mean when you say...
- Tell me how that idea is similar to/different from...
- I'm intrigued by/interested in/wondering about...
- Have you considered looking at it this way...
- Have you thought about using some of this information to help you develop your ideas...

Probing Questions to Activate Meaningful Conversations to Understand Why

- Why do you think this is the case?
- What do you think would happen if...?
- What sort of impact do you think...?
- How did you organize your information? Your thinking?
- How did you decide...?
- How did you determine...?
- How did you conclude...?
- What is the connection between... and...?
- What if the opposite were true?
- What might this or that type of person think about that?

Chapter 6

THE ART OF ACTIVE LISTENING TO UNDERSTAND AND EMPATHIZE WITH OTHERS

Cultivate Empathy-Based Conversations to Generate Action-Based Results

BUILDING AN EMPATHETIC WORKFORCE

An empathetic workforce values and shows empathy—to everyone: peers, subordinates, and supervisors. Empathy is important in workplace relationships because it helps organizations to recruit and create more effective managers and executives capable of advancing their organizations through both good and bad times. (COVID-19 as a prime example.) This means looking beyond conventional management development techniques and building the critical competencies for success. Perhaps unexpectedly, one of those abilities is empathy—a critical leadership competence.

Empathetic leadership is being able to comprehend the needs of others and being cognizant of their emotions and thoughts. Regrettably, it has long been a neglected soft skill as a performance indicator. However, CCL research indicates that today's successful leaders must be more "person-focused" and able to collaborate effectively with members of diverse teams, departments, nations, cultures, and backgrounds.

One of the most proven elements of effective leadership that has a lasting effect on the performance of the whole school system or business entity is when a leader models emotional intelligence (EQ), of which empathy is an important part.

What is EQ? Emotional intelligence is the ability to perceive emotions, access and generate emotions to assist thought, understand emotions and emotional knowledge, and reflectively regulate emotions to promote emotional and intellectual growth. Today, creative schools and educational organizations incorporate emotional intelligence into their educational systems. It is becoming abundantly clear that EQ capabilities are one of the pillars of effective leadership. EQ drives high-performance teams and its educators and students in a classroom setting.

Almost anyone can learn how to use EQ to form more useful relationships. For adolescents, EQ enhances academic achievement, helps to build relationships, and reduces risky behavior.

Adults need EQ expertise to advance in their careers and partnerships.

High EQ also has health benefits. Emotional intelligence has been linked to increased protection against heart disease, improved management of type 2 diabetes, and aides with other chronic diseases. Emotional intelligence contributes to psychological well-being, and people with poor EQ are at an increased risk of developing depression and anxiety disorders. On average, older people have a greater ability to manage their emotions and a higher level of emotional intelligence, but emotional intelligence may also be enhanced via emotional skills training.

What techniques are useful for learning how to more efficiently affect and control emotions? *A Case For EQ in Our Schools* from 6 Seconds Research explains what many researchers, psychologists, parents, and other observers have believed for a long time: People who are most successful in relationships have strongly developed interpersonal and social skills. Many leading psychologists and scholars now accept that the EQ is a form of intelligence distinct from intelligence (IQ). EQ has characteristics distinct from conventional personality tests.

According to *Psychology Today*, intelligence is "...a construct comprised of problem-solving ability, spatial manipulation abilities, and language learning." The American Psychological Association defines intelligence as "all about how well our intellect operates," which is frequently quantified through IQ testing. IQ scores are not the be all and end all of intelligence. Regardless of how many languages you study, how much material you retain, or even how efficiently you solve arithmetic problems, intelligence is a more complex metric. Regrettably, IQ and technical abilities can only take you so far.

Two unquantifiable intelligences are critical for success at the executive level in business, and even innovation, as demonstrated by in a recent *Fast Company* article on why venture investors look at one of these unquantifiable intelligences: innovation agents. Emotional Intelligence (EQ) and Social Intelligence (SI) are the two types of intelligence (SQ).

Leaders must demonstrate their empathy—that they care for every person within the business or organization. When people feel cared for, it increases positive feelings, which in turn makes their jobs more enjoyable. Given that we spend one-third of our lives at work, it stands to reason that positive experiences with coworkers will make our jobs more enjoyable. The more positive coworkers are with one another, the more open-minded they will be about each others' ideas. This makes brainstorming sessions more successful, and it encourages people to consider new ideas. This level of teamwork is required for teams to strengthen, develop, and innovate. When employees see the benefits of working together in this way, a company's productivity and performance rise and soar.

This is why, in order to create a culture of collaboration, a solid foundation of empathy-based coaching and active listening must be modeled and practiced daily. Building relationships is critical for fostering trust and facilitating the creation of a more compassionate learning community.

How Can I Listen Better?

I think that an important reason to listen well is because emotional intelligence might help us cope with stress. High EQ helps us to juggle those "glass balls", and helps us prioritize the ones that we have to drop. After all, accurate evaluation is one of the essential intelligence results (be it emotional or mathematical). Here are a few techniques for emotional intelligence while you listen:

1. Engage in imagination and curiosity

Researcher Marco Laboboni provided insights on the connections between imagination and empathy from a recent piece in *Forbes* on the neuroscience of empathy. When you imagine what someone else is thinking, you construct and build new neural learning pathways within your big beautiful brain. You don't know what people's experiences are, but you may play, "what if." "What if at this time I had to talk to me? "What if she is unsure and requires my assistance?" "What if I don't perceive a true problem?" These questions ignite your curiosity and show you to be a great listening companion.

2. Re-prioritize

Perhaps the largest hurdle is "being too busy." We LOVE to be busy! Some of us are even addicted to the physical state of it. Yet the "crazy busy" saying that we hear from many individuals, or even catch ourselves saying, is an existence so many of us complain about. I truly believe it is almost entirely self-imposed. So how do we get out of the "crazy busy" trap? Well, we find ways to be a better listener by re-prioritizing our commitment to listening. I find I am a wonderful listener on lengthy national flights, or when going on impromptu walks with a family member or a friend, or when I am surrounded by people who make me feel safe and secure and welcome me to the conversation. These are interactions with no planned agenda, and we can engage in listening with no commitments or time constraints.

The obvious conclusion is that I am a much better listener when there are NOT more important things to do. Now just take a moment and let that sink in. So, what is our responsibility as leaders? Isn't the most essential and crucial element to lead people?

3. Keep in mind that faking it, well, is just plain faking it.

Many people recognize a lot of falsifications when we interact with a fake or forced smile, or overextend a gesture to fake happiness. We convey a mixed emotional message when we "fake it." This inconsistency is a signal that might induce suspicion—even if we don't know it.

Continue to notice your own feelings. You are unlikely to be a good listener if you are exhibiting emotional feelings of impatience, worry, or overwhelm. These are not negative or bad emotions. They have a vital function and purpose, yet it is unlikely that you will be an effective listener if you ignore these emotions. Take ownership of your feelings instead so that you can be true to yourself and others.

FREE JOURNAL PAGES

Test your knowledge and see if you can detect a "Spot The Fake Smile" through this free BBC experiment.

4. Suspend and attend.

When Mimi Frenette was teaching EQ skills to the US Navy, she used the term "suspend and attend." Suspend means to cease completing other activities as well as mental chatter (e.g., thinking about what you're going to say in response). Attend is to pay attention—not merely hearing the words but paying attention to their meaning.

Leaders who listen pause in their work. Examples of this include closing their laptop, or relocating to a new chair for better sight and to help maintain their focus for active listening. When we "suspend and attend," listening becomes a physical investment in the relationship. It is the ultimate investment in trust.

Other suggestions for active listening include: Try your best not to interrupt others. Don't dismiss anyone's concerns outright. Don't be too quick to provide advice; listen first to understand, and allow individuals to have their moment in time. We can all work on these strategies.

It's also important to learn how our peers think and to understand how they work best. Inquire about their thoughts on a subject of concern. Ask what motivates them outside of work. You must understand more about what your colleagues are really interested in, and then explore how they can help you "think like an entrepreneur and design like an engineer or an artist" in order to be a part of a creative solution.

One of the most important benefits to empathy is that it builds trust. How does your organization currently build trust among its team members? When people have confidence in one another, they are able to take chances and be honest with one another. As trust grows, more information, sentiments, and opinions will be shared. The more information exchanged, the simpler it is to relate to and empathize with one another.

Building trust requires time and effort. It encompasses everyone in the group, which may include a classroom or even an entire school for your children or K-12 staff! How can you establish confidence inside your program? It all begins with trust.

Educational organizations can create workplace trust in a variety of ways, but it does not happen overnight. It takes time for K-12 students, faculty, and leaders to share their learning stories, witness the credibility of the follow-up, and value the contributions of all members.

A leader must be seen as trustworthy. You do that in several key ways: By doing what you say you will do, upholding obligations, keeping personal information private, and not speaking negatively about employees in front of others.

It also helps to build trust when leaders share their own learning stories of hardship and achievement when facilitating a new endeavor or when faced with a loss. This builds a base of trust and cultivates empathy-filled experiences. This also demonstrates that leaders, too, are human. It shows how we overcame obstacles and persevered to accomplish goals.

The trust-building process must also be reciprocal. It's important to allow colleagues to exchange information about themselves, such as their hobbies, childhood, family situation, and hometown. When you get them to learn something intimate about each other, they can relate as people. This will increase empathy and social–emotional awareness.

DYNAMIC DUO PARTNER TALKS: WHAT'S YOUR STORY?

You may want to introduce a creative active listening exercise called "Dynamic Duo Partner Talks: What's Your Story?" to articulate and represent your unique story, learn from your peers, and create stronger dynamic collaboration among your team.

Now, let's think outside the box and design your next team meeting as a joint collaboration with the staff, using group building facilitation activities and this "Unique Individual YOU" practice. First use the 6 Hat Thinking research and graphic to define your learning personality trait, and then you will participate in a design challenge to create a K-Cup "thinking hat" activity that best represents the real individual you! Participants will create, express and draw on their 6 hat K-cup who they are as individuals and what unique characteristics and traits they bring with them to represent their best selves! Then, form collaboration teams, including each thinking hat color and place in "color alike groups" or differentiated colors into each group, to create dynamic learning communities focused on various personality traits.

6 HAT THINKING

Visit the 6 Hat Thinking supportive site to learn more ways groups can use this strategy to plan thinking processes in detail and, in doing so, think together more effectively.

Next, pose a school or business challenge that you are attempting to overcome in a brainstorming exercise, keeping in mind that everybody has a seat and a voice at the table to reflect upon using their thinking hat voice, and keeping in mind their unique personality traits. Teams place their solutions on a big piece of paper with Post-it notes. Finally, give each participant two sticky dots and have them vote for their favorite two proposals that resonated with them. I hope you enjoy this activity.

It is impressive how many visual and tactile learning exercises can get colleagues to appreciate the gifts of intellect and value each person brings to the workplace. One program that I have used with educator teams is mobile scavenger hunts. This learning experience highlights unique contributions people or a group can make. For example, a person who may not be good at physical challenges can still contribute by their strength in word games, brain puzzles, or other mental activities. If you are interested, try a staff mobile scavenger hunt with Goose Chase EDU. They have great staff and student professional learning collections already designed that can easily be tweaked. You can use it as a team building strategy in your staff meeting tomorrow!

So, you can see how understanding a person encourages empathy. Often it only takes a simple question to open up creative discussions and discoveries about the people you work with on a daily basis. Here is wonderful list of questions I use in many of my leadership training sessions. Pick from there and learn something new about a co-worker.

- What event do you remember most fondly from elementary or high school?
- Who was your favorite elementary school teacher and why?
- What's a favorite family memory that has stuck with you into your adult life? Why?
- How do you use the information that you learned in your favorite class in your life today?
- What spectator activities do you most enjoy attending and watching?
- What was the most memorable event that you experienced in college?
- What is the most memorable vacation you've taken?

- What's rocking your world this month?
- What's the craziest thing you've done in your life?
- What's your favorite activity to do locally and why?
- Can you share three things about you that you think no one here knows?
- What was your least favorite class in college and why?
- What part of your current job is your favorite?
- Share one thing that you love to do that you get to do nearly every day.
- What's your most significant current challenge?
- What would you like to accomplish in your job this year?
- What is your favorite local restaurant and the meal you most enjoy eating when there?
- What outdoor activities do you most enjoy? How often do you get time to participate?
- What goal do you plan to accomplish to leave your legacy of good during your lifetime?
- What is your dream vacation?
- If money was not a consideration, what kind of a car would you buy?
- What do you enjoy in your favorite breakfast that you make at home?
- What is the best meal that you have made for dinner?
- If you could only travel to one more country, which would you choose?
- What's your favorite color and why did you pick it over all of the other choices?
- If you had the opportunity to adopt a pet, what kind of a pet would you get and why?
- When you think of the behavior of your coworkers, what behavior tends to drive you the craziest?
- What are the characteristics of the best visionary leader you ever had?
- What is your favorite activity in your current job? How often do you get to do it?
- If money were not a consideration, how would you spend the days of your life?

Another way to learn about other people is by using personality tests, such as the Myers-Briggs Type Indicator or the Strength Deployment Inventory. They can reveal similarities and variations between peers so that they can better understand the contributions that each individual makes to the team.

Another important facet to the empathetic leader is simply availability. Leaders must be available to their teams. Especially in tough times, leaders must realize that people experience challenges, and they need your help to overcome the barriers they face. You can do this by providing a mix of networking methods that are consistent with the messaging of deliverables in the workplace, as well as a variety of strategies to attract all learners. Here are some examples

- Voxer is walkie talkie chat app. It provides real-time threaded conversations where you can quickly converse with colleagues and ask for help or guidance. I have also used Voxer for interactive book club chats and working out an Innovators' Compass on a long car ride with team members in different locations to solve for a new solution or strategy.
- Marco Polo video chats are a great way to leave messages so you can read the facial clues and tone of the person you are interacting with.
- Clubhouse drop-in audio chats are similar to Voxer chats, purposeful and thoughtful conversations or teaching and learning practices.
- Micro-Podcasting with Mote extension is a great tool that can be embedded into the Google Workplace applications to leave prerecorded messages so digital markups of text are not taken out of context. The inflection in your voice helps the user read the tone of the message request or comment.
- Digitized QR/AR/VR interactive e-newsletters, such as "Learning in Loo" created by Kathleen Kersznowski, an EdTech leader in New Jersey, are a creative way to connect and make communication a priority to keep staff updated with new tools, workshops, and important need to know insights from the K-12 perspective.
- KISS meetings: 15-minute face-to-face staff meetings, "Keep it short and simple"

- Email: Remember less is more when it comes to email, so be mindful of your colleagues' time needs. Make your contact and workflow efficient with a personalized learning impact.

One critical time to establish empathy and trust is to share when you are excited about being correct or when you receive support from others. Yet it is just as important to remember to confront and identify gaps when you're incorrect. For example, let's say you misrepresented a date or time for a critical event in the monthly newsletter. It is important to own up to the mistake ASAP and take step to ensure it does not happen again, as actions speak louder than words. This will result in more constructive engagement in open forums, which will promote positive reform within the business company, the school, and society.

Knowledge of yourself is essential for inventive problem solving. Do you get flustered and stressed easily? Restrain yourself. When things get difficult, recognize and regulate your breathing to stay calm. Identify your stress triggers and learn how to anticipate them to sustain your leadership presence.

As you develop your own empathy and model it to develop your team's empathy, it's important to coach and model the strategies that result in an effective change to improve your organization. Monitor your leadership development through a weekly reflection journal or checklist. You could review your action focused leadership strategies with a peer, so you can realize when it's successful, which will boost your leadership morale and your rapport with colleagues.

A final important piece to developing empathy is remembering to celebrate often to build your team. One way to do this is ending each quarter, semester, or year with "Your Greatest Contribution." To do this, partner each participant with a teammate. Ask each team member to explain her most important contribution to the team and how it strengthened a teaching, learning, or leadership practice. Then, the teammate offers a piece of advice. For example, she might suggest that her team member takes her contribution to the next level. Then the team members switch roles. A skilled facilitator is needed to direct this practice.

Trust is the cornerstone for every company and organization to succeed. Trust takes time and commitment to create, nurture, and sustain. This is not to suggest that there will be no disputes. However, disputes can be handled in a balanced, proactive manner. Leaders who model empathy and trust develop strong communities. The benefits can be enormous.

UNDERSTANDING BODY LANGUAGE

Every conversation provides an active listening opportunity to gain a new viewpoint from the perspective of others. Our big beautiful brains learn to enjoy new ideas through impressionism, while also instilling and applying deeper empathy and empathic ability to better understand each other and our world. Each time we seek out connection and communication shows our true calling to lead in our personal and professional lives.

To become a better active listener, you need to listen to more than just words. You need to learn how to understand body language. Our bodies communicate volumes by making eye contact (or not!), by standing up straight (or slouching), and by holding your head high (or casting your face down). Nonverbal signals such as voice tone, facial expressions, gestures, and posture all play a role in communication.

People judge your competence in a fraction of a second. They assess your integrity based on far more than just what you say.

By learning to understand both verbal and nonverbal communication, you can become better at "reading the room" and understanding when to be a spectator and when to be a participant. With these skills, you'll be well on the way to more creative, fruitful, and solution-oriented discussions. Let's take a close look at body language and how it can help you better understand and communicate with people.

What is body language? Simply put, body language is the unspoken element of communication with which we communicate our thoughts and emotions. Sometimes our body language communicates more authentic, honest thoughts than our actual words do. An example of body language is a relaxed facial expression that breaks into a genuine smile—with your lips pulled up and your brows wrinkled. Another example of body language is a head tilt to suggest listening, as my youngest son Jacob often does. A third is sitting or standing upright to show interest.

If you can understand other people's body language, you will be better able to comprehend the whole message that they are trying to convey. Then in reaction to their communication, you'll be able to change your own body language to express what you are hoping to convey.

POWER AND INFLUENCE

Deborah Gruenfeld, a Stanford Professor of Leadership and Organizational Behavior at the Stanford Graduate School of Business, Co-director of the Executive Program for Women Leaders, introduces you to the body languages of force and authority and teaches you how to use them efficiently. This is particularly important for women, who face more gender discrimination at work. Gruenfeld also shares cutting-edge cognitive science findings into how body language shapes your own psychology.

Please take time to review this discussion guide of "Power and Influence" to improve your presence with leadership body language, and the physical messages that you are signaling to your colleagues and teammates.

We communicate using words, gestures, signs, and expressions. It is difficult to remain silent. In the 1970s, professor of psychology Albert Mehrabian investigated the relevance of non-verbal communication and the impact of contradictory messages to gain a better understanding of communication. The impact of non-verbal communication is more than previously believed.

An example of contradictory messages is someone pounding their feet and screaming "I'm not furious" Does he appear credible? Albert Mehrabian established the 7-38-55 rule of Communication, demonstrating that just 7 percent of what we say is literal. The use of one's voice, including tone, intonation, and loudness, accounts for 38 percent of communication, while body language accounts for up to 55 percent. Along the same lines is the Mehrabian's Relationship Model, which notes body language is more important than tone of voice and word choice to express emotions. This helps to understand why it's so difficult to gauge a person's mood when you can't see her, for example, when using email or texting.

Learning to read body language is important for leaders because managing difficult interactions is a necessary part of leadership. You might have to deal with a difficult customer, give negative feedback to a person, or negotiate a sticky contract. These conditions are often aggravated by feelings of nervousness, exhaustion, or anger. No matter how hard we try to hide these emotions, they are still conveyed in our body language.

For example, here are some body language signals that communicate a person is disengaged, disinterested, or dissatisfied.

- Arms folded over the chest
- Lips tensed
- Body shifted away from you
- Hands avoiding touch
- Eyes downcast
- Restlessness, such as tapping feet

On the other hand, more open body language communicates that your mindset is open as well. It can actually prevent you from transmitting opposing messages. Here are some ways from the Mind Tools website that your body language can project self-assurance and clarity. By changing your body language, you can make a better first impression.

- Maintain an open stance. Be at ease, but don't slouch. Place your hands at your sides and sit or stand straight. (Standing with your hands on your hips can convey anger or an urge to conquer.)
- Use a strong handshake. (But not an aggressive one, which might make the person feel uncomfortable.)
- Maintain continuous eye contact. Try to keep the other person's eyes on you for a few seconds at a time. This will convey to them that you are genuine and dedicated. (Don't make it a staring contest.)
- Keep your hands away from your ears, nose, and hair. (Touching your face can make you seem dishonest or untrustworthy.)

With this basic body language knowledge, you will be better and quicker at reading any room. It can take time and practice, but in time paying attention to body language will become a habit. This will help you to become a better leader. Also, you will begin to pay more attention to your own body language—what your body is communicating for you. This will help you as a leader communicate more effectively to your team.

Emotional intelligence is emerging as a critical factor in sustaining high achievement, retention, and positive actions, as well as improving life success. Schools, educational institutions, and corporations are gradually turning to EQ to optimize student and social outcomes, such as school attrition, student satisfaction, peer relationships, and health.

What is the root of this change? Is EQ intelligence a fad, or does study produce new ideas and resources with a real impact on performance? And, if EQ is so important, how do educational officials, teachers, and students improve it?

Read this school case study from 6 Seconds, which I refer to in all of my Social Emotional Learning (SEL) courses for adult learners. It will assist you in identifying two or three EQ areas that will help you sustain your visionary roadmap while you develop your leadership trust and presence. If you'd like practice to make EQ permanent in your life, checkout this daily dose of vitamin EQ calendar challenges to improve your well-being from All Things EQ: http://www.allthingseq.com/

As an additional EQ resource, you might enjoy this web resource from the InspirED project https://eq.org/learn/courses/inspired/ in partnership with Facebook and the Yale Center for Emotional Intelligence. This educational leadership toolbox offers a host of powerful tips and strategies to:

- Practice emotional intelligence for yourself as an educational leader
- Apply emotional intelligence to strengthen student and collegial relationships
- Supercharge your classroom or staff in-services with emotional intelligence strategies

HAND SIGNALS

People naturally gesture with their hands, making hand movements a familiar form of body language. Consider these common signals:

- Thumbs up = okay
- Two fingers up = peace or goodwill
- Index finger up = wait or I have a question
- High five = I need your full attention
- Palms up = what?

I often use these hand gestures to communicate nonverbally and I encourage my students and colleagues to do the same. I have adopted these five hand singles from one of my favorite educational leadership organizations known as Edutopia. You can watch their video here.

Finally, I recently enrolled in Google Grow's free Coursera course The Science of Well Being, https://www.coursera.org/learn/the-science-of-well-being, and I am gaining another qualification as a micro-credential to continue to develop my leadership confidence, social emotional well-being, and presence with others. Every day, I aspire to be my best self and share my optimistic genius with others, which means I must continue to learn and invest in myself. Others view me as remaining on top of my leadership game as a result of these modeled acts of self-directed continued development, and it also illustrates that life upskilling is an important leadership trait to lead a team with dignity, credibility, and sound analysis to enhance the learning atmosphere for everyone involved. I enjoy learning, and the outcomes inform my leadership innovative roadmap. This is why you should prioritize your learning commitment in yourself. It can evolve and foster more empathy-based interactions with your peers, resulting in action-based outcomes, as you listen to and learn from your teammates. You can find all of the free Google Grow courses and low-cost certifications to help you grow your talents, career, and business at https://grow.google.com

Putting Purpose into Practice

DISCOVER YOUR CREATIVE TYPE

Who doesn't love a good personality test!? The Adobe Creative Type is a quick assessment that delves into different aspects of your creative personality. The test, which is based on psychological testing, assesses your fundamental behaviors and tendencies—how you think, behave, and see the world—to help you better understand who you are. In just a few minutes, you'll gain a better understanding of your motives, plus insight into how to optimize your talents and face your challenges. Spend a few minutes exploring the Adobe Creative Type website to discover the one-of-a-kind person that you are!

These personality styles are not binary classifications. Consider them to be signposts leading you in the direction of your full artistic ability. Though you are most likely one of the core styles, you can change types at various points in your life and career or at different stages in the creative process. You have a little bit of each of the eight forms inside you as a creative.

Share your observations with a peer, discuss your similarities and differences, and see if you may be able to work on the next project together based on your creative types.

Ask yourself these questions:

- How might a small collaborative adjustment encourage you to learn more about yourself?
- Will getting to know yourself better help you develop confidence and rapport with your team?
- How could sharing your learning interests and excitement with a colleague help you build more trust in your working relationships?

IMPROVE YOUR SELF-CARE

When you combine new understanding about your personality with recognizing the critical value of self-care, you will discover an optimal wellness alignment between your everyday tasks, family and life obligations, and career expectations. With this in mind, it is vital that we identify helpful methods for managing our priorities when tackling projects of any size. We will easily get frustrated by tension and anxiety if we don't have a strategy in place. We may also feel a tremendous amount of responsibility placed on ourselves, and we may be unsure how to cross the finish line in a constructive manner. These stresses can cause mood swings, which can lead to negative work-related emotions and ill-fated job results. This in turn can be reflected onto coworkers who seem to be working at a higher pace or at a more profitable level than you are. If we do not strike the right balance, it will lead to work, family, and life burnout. (See the section about burnout on page 115.)

Knowing that you have power over whatever situation you face will help you react and respond to others as you tackle the tasks at hand. We become even stronger leaders when we lead by example and verbalize how to manage these uncharted territories, such as when changing a project's workflow or when things go wrong and tension sets in. This is why it is important to model and monitor our own workplace challenging habits, so that we can lead by example and share our milestones with peers, letting them know we too are human while still providing a learning opportunity. Documenting and focusing on difficult circumstances enables you and your colleagues to deal with, resolve, and support constructive workplace recovery strategies.

FREE JOURNAL PAGES

Please make a copy and consult with this self-care action template to assist you in identifying helpful solutions and a course of action for identifying stress and anxiety causes linked to incidents in your own life. When you are at ease, share your learning insights with a colleague or a friend on how you have been more aware about what triggers your tension, and celebrate your effective approaches to regaining control of your self-care agenda to achieve an optimal work-life-family balance. The self-care action template will also help you deal with stress by reminding you of meditation and awareness practices.

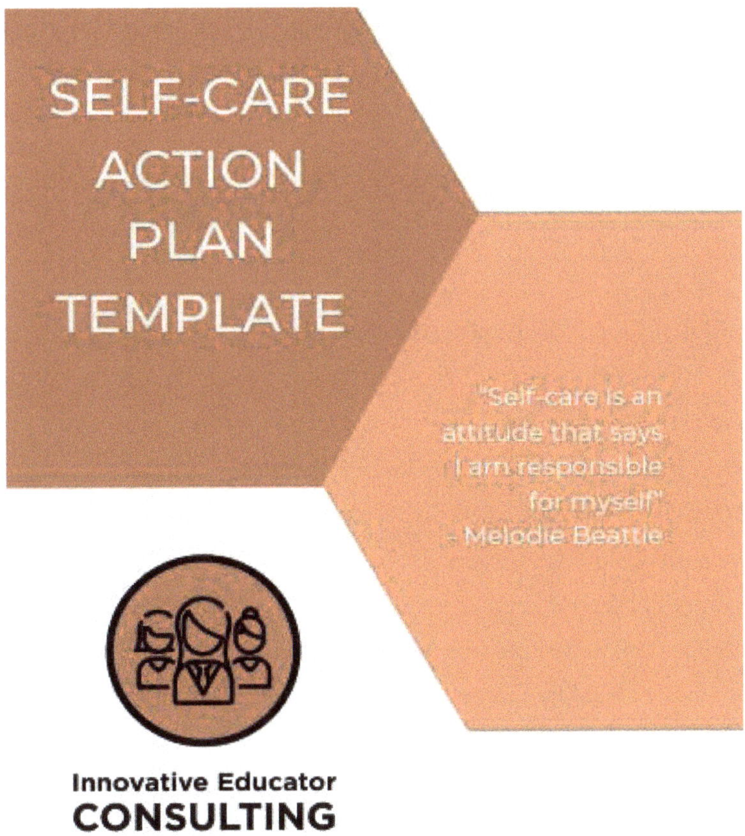

Chapter 7

THE PURSUIT OF HAPPINESS

Enjoy Professional Achievement and Personal Fulfillment Without Feeling Guilty

FINDING BALANCE TO HONOR PROFESSIONAL AND PERSONAL LEARNING

"Balance" is the word of the year. We've heard the word many times during the global pandemic. But what does it actually mean to *balance* our lives, families, and careers? Is "balance" a buzzword that everybody is obsessed about, with some mastering it and others failing?

For me, I have to really focus on balancing my life, making it important to me personally and professionally. For me to maintain balance, I need to have a work-life-family balance action plan in place as well as a thoughtful micro-blog, as my reflection journal to share what is working, what is not working, what I need to change, the big crazy ideas I come up with, and to take time to celebrate the moments of success.

Visualizing a physical calender is key for me to organize myself and maintain balance in all facets of my life. I use a paper calender, because if I don't see a visual picture or list, events and tasks can easily fall by the wayside.

Sometimes, I take on too much, burn the candle at both ends, and don't have a good work-life-family balance.

A tool that can help you achieve balance is a vision board. (See "Putting Purpose into Practice: Create Your Vision Board" on page 31.) This will help you to visualize what balance looks like to you. You can use your vision board as a springboard to create a roadmap with essential measures to take action and make your dreams a reality.

An important part of achieving balance is learning how to say no. We must understand that it is appropriate to say no. It's impossible to say yes to everything. Saying no can help you achieve balance. Saying no can also help the person you're saying no to. In fact, saying no to someone can empower them in new ways.

Many women leaders fear that saying no will degrade their work, family, and friend relationships. We've been taught to always say yes and give our best all of the time. Saying no makes us feel guilty. These feelings of guilt get in our way.

I found it extraordinarily difficult to say no to almost every request given to me during my early years as a mom, wife, nana to four grandchildren, and then once again at the very beginning of the start of my women-in-leadership company. Even if a demand didn't pique my curiosity, I felt obligated to do it anyway. It took me twice as long to finish the assignment because I was unmotivated or uninterested in planning the product or presentation. Finally after I completed the Cornell University Women-in-Leadership Executive Administration program in 2018, I realized the importance of prioritizing my personal and professional work-life-family balance. Even though I had many requests to present locally, nationally, and internationally at EdTech conferences, I had to prioritize which events mattered the most.

Even when some of the requests were not really in my wheelhouse, and placed me in an awkward work zone at times, I knew it was all part of growing my big beautiful brain and helping me develop my leadership skills. I realize now that saying yes to anything and everything made it impossible for me to maintain my work-life-family balance, and it really cut into my sleep at times. I was working too hard, overtired all the time, and stressed out. I couldn't find time to exercise, which has always been a stress outlet for me.

I took a step back and reevaluated my visionary roadmap and mission. I asked myself, *Where is this road I'm on taking me?* I didn't feel well about the amount of work that I was doing. Due to the extreme stress, I gained about 15 pounds in two years. It was a cortisol reaction: Think of cortisol as nature's built-in alarm system. When you feel stressed, cortisol boosts your energy so you can cope. Cortisol also works with certain parts of your brain to control your mood, motivation, and fear.

At that time, some of the projects I was stressing out about weren't even of the highest importance to me. That's when I realized I'd been sidetracked by work. I discovered that some of my sadness was linked to the imbalance between my personal and professional life. I had some more in-depth soul-searching talks with my amazing team. I felt comfortable confiding in them, and they were eager to share with me their outlooks and strategies on maintaining their own work-life-family balance.

They instructed, coached, and mentored me on several activities to help me regain my balance. I found that I was happiest writing and designing content that engaged the whole learning with a foundation of SEL and hands-on learning techniques to personalize the learning experience. They also made me understand that I couldn't create and fulfill every job. I needed to delegate some of those assignments to consultants. They assured me that it would be fine to delegate these responsibilities, and that it also would be fine if I was not in complete control of everything all of the time. This was an epiphany for me.

I was delighted to find that delegating tasks reduced my workload. I was surprised to discover that handing over these tasks to my team members, motivated them, and the projects benefitted by having their fresh outlooks. The end results were often 10 times better than my original ideas were!

This is when I knew I must truly strike a different balance. I needed to let go of the micromanaging mentality and invest in my team. Once I let go of some of the responsibility, I realized it felt nice. I recognized that my consultants are incredibly trustworthy and extremely imaginative. I knew that I could inspire them with these new demanding challenges that were truly in their wheelhouses with their skills. My stress and tension began to dissipate. I realized that everything was going to be okay. My servant leadership vision really kicked into high gear, and I finally found a way to balance my career success and my personal life—without feeling guilty.

Overachievers are particularly prone to burnout. There people react to job stress by doing more work, which can be exacerbated by a workplace in which top performers regularly take on the most demanding tasks as well as extra duties such as mentoring lower-level workers. This list of goals can be used to develop balanced strategies:

- Avoid having to compensate the overachiever for the sake of others. Enable the best performers to partner with colleagues who are at or above the capacity level. This allows the project's workload and demands to be more distributed and shared, as well as the opportunity to learn and improve. Having to take up the slack and/or mentor lower performers on a daily basis depletes a high performer's energy and morale.
- Allow allowances for high-performing workers. Most executives assume that their managers just take on the most demanding assignments. This may be true in some cases, but over time, the individual may move farther away from the location he or she desired. The leader will be shocked to hear which tasks a high-performing employee loves working on.
- Wait for the "Yes" crowd. Overachievers may agree to any application because they believe it is requested of them, they have trouble saying "no," or they disregard the time and energy required. Employees who keep promising to do only one more thing may feel like they'll never catch up, that they're unsuccessful, and that they're not measuring up to standards. These thoughts will contribute to burnout.

Creating a workplace plan is a realistic method for aiding an employee who is suffering burnout. As part of every program, ask the employee if they would like to be recognized for their accomplishments and victories. This may include immediate and personal kudos, prospects for growth and development, public appreciation, or financial rewards. It is important to consider what the employee values the most. Employees who are burned out and have a major lack of faith in their overall competency can benefit from this. Accept ways for the employee to assist or help others, but bear in mind that this might not be a successful idea if this was a routine and unpleasant aspect of the employee's role prior to burnout. You may help alleviate apathy and cynicism by diverting focus away from something they are not doing well and instead leveraging their skills to mentor or coach someone else.

The development of a workplace plan is a hands-on solution to supporting an employee who is suffering burnout. As part of this approach, remind staff of their milestones and achievements. This may include immediate gratitude, opportunities for development and progress, public attention, or incentives. It is important to consider what the employee values the most. This will help personnel recognize burnout causes and regions of lack of faith in their general abilities. Consider the workers' opportunities to help or encourage others, bearing in mind that this would not be an optimal solution because it was a repetitive and demanding place of employment before they were stressed out. You can help to alleviate apathy and cynicism by taking the emphasis off what they don't do well by using their influence to mentor or coach another human.

If you are searching for more approaches and tactics to direct your efforts with employee or colleague burnout, please visit the website Workplace Strategies for Mental Health for more accommodation strategies to better improve employee engagement and prevent burnout.

How can you find your own balance? Begin by having some conversations with yourself, asking: What parts of my life are in balance? What parts are not in balance? Am I doing too much of one type of thing—and sacrificing another? Do I say yes too much? All of the time? What can I say no to or delegate to someone else?

Next talk with your family, friends, and colleagues. What do they observe about your balance? Sometimes people close to us can see things about us we cannot. Your closest colleagues might be able to assist you in identifying solutions to find a healthier balance in your life. It often begins by prioritizing what is most important and purposeful in life that you want to achieve.

Sometimes in life, we might get thrown off balance by taking a wrong turn that leads to a happy adventure, but it can also derail us and drive us into a rabbit hole that leads to a total lost cause. Having awareness that you've lost your balance, doing some soul-searching, and then talking with close friends can help you to get back on track and rebalance your life.

The best way to maintain balance is to keep aware of your priorities. I do this by making a to-do list and then identifying the top three priorities on the list. As I complete tasks, I check them off the list. This gives me a feeling of accomplishment and reduces my mental workload.

Making a checklist also helps me to recognize items on my list that I can delegate to a team member or pass to a colleague who might be better suited to it. Perhaps a task complements her wheelhouse better than mine, and she might be able to complete it more effectively than me. I find it very rewarding to share a task with a team member or colleague. I might still be able to supervise or assist, and they receive a creative challenge for which they can share their skills with others.

INVESTING IN YOURSELF: HEALTHY BOUNDARIES AND SELF-COMPASSION

We've talked about strategies to be your best self every day and finding your balance. We talked about finding happiness. Next, we'll take things a step forward and talk about why we need to invest in ourselves by setting strong boundaries and practicing self-compassion.

Healthy Boundaries

To maintain balance in our lives, we can't say yes to everything. Sometimes, you might want to say yes, such as when you owe someone a favor or when you have free time and would like to assist. Other times, however, you might not want to say yes. You have the right to say no, and you have the right not to feel bad about it. You can't please everybody all of the time. If you're patient and reasonable when saying no, there should be no issues. If issues arise, through clear communication, they usually can be resolved quickly.

A tool that you can use to help define for you when and how to say yes—or no—is to set physical and mental boundaries. Limiting oneself is an important aspect of shaping one's identity and is essential for one's mental stability and well-being. An example of a physical boundary a home office space where you complete your business or work tasks, that is far away from your family entertaining and relaxation area. Another way to set a boundary is to set a timer to remind yourself to take a break from your work and go outside a for quick walk, drink some water, and do something fun!

Emotional boundaries are where you have locked in a go-to response of when to say no and when to say yes to work requests that fulfill your happiness bucket. It also means identifying and prioritizing personal self-care as a routine to relax, calm your big beautiful brain to stay creative, and enjoy life's moments that bring you joy.

Boundaries can be loose or rigid, with healthy boundaries often falling right in the middle. Healthy boundaries are an essential component of self-care. This is because poor limits, whether at work or in our personal relationships, lead to frustration, anger, and burnout.

Boundaries support people in two ways. First, they give us permission to say no, to refrain from taking on something new. They help us hear requests as questions, to which we can say no, rather than as demands, to which we have to say yes.

Second, boundaries create a line between what is acceptable and unacceptable to us. Although some behaviors clearly offend nearly all, we all have differing degrees of pleasure with everything from intimacy and privacy to tardiness. When someone responds in a way that does not sound right to us—when they cross our line—we must protect ourselves by informing them and making that line more visible. If we don't, we could get resentful or break down and leave the relationship—as I did from the K-12 service agency.

The future belongs to those who believe in the beauty of their dreams.
—Eleanor Roosevelt

Setting limits helps leaders prevent burnout and remain in the field for a longer period of time. This is important because it implies that successful job restrictions help people gain greater happiness and less stress in their work lives, helping them to have better personal lives.

On the other hand, failing to establish healthy boundaries can cause uncertainty, financial burdens, wasted time, and relationship issues, which may cause emotional distress. To put it another way, a violation of reasonable boundaries can have a negative effect on all aspects of a person's life. Setting good limits can have a range of benefits, such as assisting people in making decisions that are better for them rather than just those around them. Having control over one's life is essential to quality self-care.

It's essential to communicate your boundaries. If people don't understand your boundaries, they might fear that they're asking too much. Or they can feel as though they are tiptoeing around you, unsure if they have offended you. Or they might unwittingly upset you by stepping over a boundary, making you upset or even angry.

How much easier would it be to ask a friend for a favor if you could trust that she'd refuse if she couldn't do it? On the other hand, how difficult is it to ask a friend for something who you worry won't speak up if she can't do it. Would you be afraid to even ask?

Boundaries make it easier and less confusing for all, resulting in closer and better relationships. However, setting boundaries isn't always easy. Even if you set boundaries and communicate them clearly, some people might still criticize you if you say no to a request. Also some people try to push boundaries to see how serious you are about holding them. Or people might use your boundaries against you, trying to get you to behave in a certain way, such as agreeing to take on everything. Some people might try to get you to avoid setting boundaries entirely.

That doesn't mean you're doing anything wrong. It could simply imply that you need to be more transparent and clear about your boundaries before other people will respect them.

Here are six tips for creating compassionate boundaries, adapted from the Dananel Counseling Group.

1. Check in with yourself and determine your goals. The first step to establish boundaries is to determine what you want, what is most essential to you, and where you want to draw the lines. Consider what *gives* you energy vs. what *drains* your energy and what makes you happy vs. what frustrates you. Recognize that every time you say yes to something, you say no to something else. Ask yourself:

- Are you creating room in your life for the things that are truly important to you?
- What would you be unable to perform if you accept this additional responsibility?

2. Allow for a brief pause. Before answering when someone asks you to do something, take a pause. Check in with yourself to discover how you truly feel. Ask yourself:

- Am I truly alright with this?
- Am I simply frightened of disappointing or offending this person?

Stop pressuring yourself to respond to requests immediately. If you're at a loss for words, simply say, "I'll have to think about that," "I'll have to get back to you," or "I need more time to think about that idea."

3. Be transparent, honest, and unafraid to say no. Being honest and frank is beneficial to your relationships—even when it's not the most comfortable thing to do. A person who made a request of you might be unhappy now if you say no, but she could be much more dissatisfied if you say yes and later loathe her for asking. A request is a question, and a perfectly acceptable response is no.

4. Try not to over-explain. You don't have to defend yourself when you give yourself freedom to create limits. In some cases, a clarification is required. In some circumstances, your limit might invite the other person to respond—or even to object. The word no is often best used to finish a statement. If you sense that you are coming across as abrupt, you could elaborate by saying something like, "I've got a lot on my plate right now, and I know I wouldn't be able to give you the time or attention this requires. However, I appreciate you thinking of me."

5. Lose the guilt. The way to avoid shame is to maintain modesty. Recognize that the vast majority of people can function without you—yes, this is true. If you say no to a person's request, she will likely seek someone else, and it's unlikely to be a huge problem. Knowing that we are not completely necessary in most situations will be quite liberating for the vast majority of us.

6. Say yes to other possibilities. Once you've said no to some requests, what do you do with the additional time in your life? Say yes to tasks that help you achieve your goals and provide you joy and fulfillment. Spend time with family and friends who mean a lot to you. Schedule time for hobbies and activities that will nourish you—rather than exhaust you. Allow yourself to be entirely immersed in the activities that give you joy. What do you want to say "amen" to today?

Putting Purpose into Practice

SET HEALTHY BOUNDARIES

Learning to show compassion and kindness to yourself is crucial in setting healthy boundaries. Check out these six boundary-setting exercises, adapted from Positive Psychology. These detailed exercises will help you set and hold healthy boundaries, and they will also give you tools to help your team members or students set and maintain their own boundaries.

1. Recognize that you cannot do everything. Insure that whatever you're saying yes to is something you have time for and, most importantly, something you really want to do. Try not to engage too many requests on a single day if you have a lot going on. If you have a free evening one day and the question is posed, you should say yes if you wish, but you should also know that it is appropriate to say no. You won't have time to do everything you want to do on a regular basis, let alone support others. Knowing that you can't do everything and that it's okay to say no to someone is very beneficial to your mental well-being and to ensure your happiness.

2. Offer an alternative. When someone makes a request and you want to say no, offer them an alternative idea. If you cannot specifically assist them, you could make a recommendation or provide a plan that can assist them. As long as you can provide something that can support the person, this is an outstanding alternative to saying no. You are still assisting the individual—even though you are not saying yes and taking up your time. This is an excellent method for saying no without feeling guilty.

3. When you say no, don't apologize. This might be difficult at first, but if you someone without apologizing, it will be much simpler. You should not need to apologize when you are unable to fulfill a job that they have requested. Apologizing implies that you are guilty of something, when saying no to anyone is nothing to feel guilty about.

4. Recognize that you have difficulties saying no. The first step is admitting that you have a problem. Understanding that you have trouble saying no will significantly assist you in coping with it. If you understand what is preventing you from saying no, you will be more realistic about the situation and see it from a different perspective. Are you scared of being judged for saying no? Perhaps you believe that the person to whom you are saying no would be offended by your decision. If this is the case, consider backing away from this relationship for a while and associating yourself with less easily offended people.

5. Recognize your worth. Is part of the reason you can't say no that you want other people's validation, or you don't want them to be irritated at you, dislike you, or feel let down by you? If so, increase your feelings of self-worth. If you depend on others' acceptance of you to boost your self-worth, you likely think their views are more important than your own. It also suggests that you are putting people ahead of yourself. You must understand your own worth. Other people's views of your strengths do not define you, nor do their views of your faults. It is appropriate to prioritize yourself and respect your own views over the opinions of others.

6. Develop a go-to phrase. Having a rehearsed expression that you can use when you're asked to do something unexpectedly is incredibly beneficial, particularly if you're not great at thinking on your feet. Try saying, "Thank you for asking, but I have other obligations, and I won't be able to support you with that." This is incredibly valuable and handy to have on hand in case you are inclined to panic when questioned on the spot.

PRIORITIZING YOUR SELF-CARE

Finding balance in your life is more important than ever when you are a leader. It is so important to take care of yourselves. Please review the following slide deck to enhance and practice prioritizing your self-care, SEL and gratitude strategies, and healthy boundary activities of reinforcements. I use this slide deck as a teaching and learning guide in all of my leadership and coaching sessions to build social emotional resilience and learning confidence in people who are looking to develop and maintain better work-home balance.

Self-Compassion

It's critical to properly take care of yourself as a leader. I practice self-compassion techniques daily to remain calm, fill my day with gratitude, and ease the stressful times, and situations I cannot control. Here are my top 10 self-compassion strategies.

1. Take a deep breath. How much do you focus on your breathing? For most people, the response is "not enough." In difficult times, your breathing might become shallow and strained. Think of a time when you were under intense pressure, such as during a confrontational conversation or when taking an exam. After the situation passed, do you remember taking a deep breath? You did that because you were holding your breath through that overwhelming period of stress. Rather than holding your breath throughout the day, try to take long, slow breaths. This will improve your mental condition and fitness. So, if you want to be well, take a deep breath!

2. Enjoy the current moment. The best gift you can give yourself is the current moment. So, let go of the past. Also, don't be worried about your concerns for tomorrow. Instead, learn how to make the best of what you do have today—the present moment.

3. Forgive yourself. Even if you are excellent at forgiving others, forgiving yourself can be much more difficult. Remember that you are human, and you will make mistakes. However, until you are able to forgive yourself for missteps and able to let them go, you're depriving yourself of potential pleasure. If you make a mistake, accept responsibility, forgive yourself, and move on.

4. Forgive others. Just as you forgive yourself, it's also important to forgive others. When you hang on to the hatred or suffering that someone has caused you, you're holding that toxic connection between you and that person as well. The only way to free yourself from those shackles for good is to forgive them fully. This can take time, so be patient with yourself. A technique I use is to give them love and let them go.

5. Surrender your decision. Learn to be more accepting of yourself and others. Our ability to see the positive in situations is clouded by judgement, whether it is about oneself, another person, or a circumstance. This can preclude you from capitalizing on opportunities that arise. Judgment will stymie your progress and push you further away from your objectives. Because decision making is discretionary, pick performance instead!

6. Be prepared for great things. Do you see the glass half-empty or half-full? Training your brain to expect the best from everything might boost your day—and also your life. Expect the best, and you are more likely to get it.

7. Invest in your relationships. It is in our essence to be sociable and check out other people's business. Think about how much time you spend with the ones who love and support you the most and bring you joy. Are you investing enough quality time with them? Make more time in your days to cultivate the relationships that are important to you.

8. Say thank you. Cultivate an attitude of gratitude. The rewards of appreciation for a happy, more fulfilling life cannot be overstated. Appreciation is the first step toward contentment—and peace.

9. Let go of the old. To make room for the things you want to come into your life, you have to get rid of some old things that no longer serve you. Ask yourself, *What obstacles are holding me back or preventing me from doing what it is that I want most?* Create room in your life for positive, optimistic learning experiences. For example, I wear an Origami Owl necklace engraved with "Let It Go" as a reminder to be kind to myself, my company, and the girls and young women leaders I mentor.

The Owlette program for girls and BROs program for boys empowers youth ages 11 to 17 to work alongside an adult, providing them with real-life experience as young entrepreneurs. Your Owlette (or BRO) will develop skills, grow confidence, and celebrate progress with you as their mentor. Although this is a jewelry company (and a pretty cool one at that!), what it's really about is sharing stories and building a network of friends and family.

10. Express love to yourself. If you want to make the best of every second, you must first begin to love yourself. Empower yourself with true love for the spirit, body, and soul, and genuinely cherish yourself. When you embrace yourself, the path of the day will naturally reshape into something you will be enthusiastic about.

Putting Purpose into Practice

DEVELOP YOUR SELF-COMPASSION ACTION PLAN

Developing a self-care action plan can greatly improve your life. Yes, it can be that easy. Why not get started today? A self care action plan can help you improve your health and wellness, manage your stress, and maintain your professionalism with your teammates. Learn to discover activities and behaviors that enhance your well-being and maintain and manage quality self-care techniques moving forward.

Chapter 8

LEAN-IN LEADERSHIP ENGAGEMENT STRATEGIES

Leaning In Makes People Feel Included and Valued

KNOWING WHEN TO LEAN IN TO SUPPORT COURAGEOUS CONVERSATIONS

In chapter 6, we reviewed and gained new insights of how to read the room by being an active listener and observer of body language, tone of voice, and reactive statements and viewpoints of critical feedback and comments. Next, I'm going to share critical insights of when to contribute and lean in with your intelligence and ideas to pursue courageous conversations and have productive, promising outcomes.

Communication seems to break down more frequently when it is most critical to meeting our goals at work or at home. When our personal or professional goals are not being met, and the communication is not working, we may become frustrated and not represent our best selves. When we don't get our way or we don't feel we are being heard or understood, we may feel hurt or angry. Difficult conversations can be frightening because the stakes are high. Disappointment has a real cost, boosting everyone's defenses.

Often during a difficult time or conversation, our instinct is to withdraw or back away. We want to avoid the conflict. However, it's during these times that it might be better to lean in. *Lean in* became a business motto in 2013, taken from the title of the book *Lean In: Women, Work, and the Will to Lead* written by Sheryl Sandberg, the Chief Operating Officer of Facebook, and Nell Scovell, a writer and Sandberg's collaborator. Sandberg's book outlines business strategies to help women achieve success, and its title perfectly paints a picture of what Sandberg believes women need to do to move up in the business world: to press ahead, to project confidence, to "sit at the table" and physically *lean in* to make herself heard.

As we become more aware of our leadership actions and cognitive presence, let's now focus on how we can wear our new leadership instructional designer hats to guide and lead us with success. Part of the lean in technique is "what" you bring to the table. This means your tone and message of delivery, your inquiry based clarifying questions, and your presentation style, techniques, and collaborative activities to engage your colleagues and teammates with new learning experiences.

You might not have considered an instructional designer hat as a leadership trait, but it projects a necessary creative flair and element of fun as you move forward with

DIFFICULT CONVERSATIONS

As a support strategy guide, and instead of recreating the wheel, I would like to share with you this Difficult Conversations Guide, created by Sheryl Sandberg's LEAN In organization and Fred Kofman, director of the Conscious Business Center at Universidad Francisco Marroquín and president of the academic board of Axialent.

This guide outlines the importance of how effective conversations go through seven critical steps in order to be effective. It also gives signs of how conversations break down due to high-stakes discussions, and how the analogy of pushing with your words is like pushing with your hands and truly projects a defensive presence and negative attitude. It also provides critical insight on three essential ingredients for a successful conversation to occur, when we purposely plan and focus on our tone and active body language of observing, how we present our physical stance to focus on the optimistic leadership outcomes, and how this lends itself the deeper impact of the conversation with taking leadership responsibility within ourselves.

implementing your go-to strategies, hands-on learning experiences and to support difficult and creative conversations.

One place it's important to lean in is during meetings you lead. It's essential to have a plan in place when meetings with your colleagues. It sets a productive tone for the conversation.

Part of your meeting plan should include inclusive openings and optimistic closings. Beginning each meeting with an inclusive opening and ending each meeting with an optimistic closing is important because people are more likely to remember the beginnings and endings of meeting—rather than the middles.

An inclusive opening is a facilitation technique to kick off your meeting with a warm welcome and acknowledge the attendees being present through a community-building activity. It's important to start with an inclusive opening because it makes the meeting attendees feel valued and included.

For my meetings, I keep the introductions of the meeting minutes as succinct as possible, noting the purpose and expected learning outcome of the meeting. When I know we need to have some team building or I anticipate a difficult conversation, I often begin meetings with an icebreaker—a getting-to-know-you activity. These communication techniques take the focus off the heavy focus and engage people in a personalized, fun dialogue to get to know each other better and to become more aware and respectful of each other.

In addition to verbally introducing attendees, you can make them feel included with respectful, open body language. You can offer them helpful feedback and validate ideas they present. It's essential to acknowledge their contributions to the team effort are valued to move forward on an idea or project.

An optimistic closing is ending the meeting on a high note. It's beneficial to do this because you want to send attendees out of your meeting feeling positive and hopeful about the meeting topic.

It's also important to close out the meeting with purpose and action steps, so that everyone feels included, knows what is expected of them, and can move forward with the collective and collaborative team vision.

Leading effective meetings is like maintaining a fine-tuned instrument. For the pitch and tone of the ensemble to be played well so everyone can enjoy the musical outcome, you need to strive to achieve that perfect melody.

THINKING ROUTINE TOOLBOX

When I really need to have a difficult meeting, I draw on Project Zero's Thinking Routine Toolbox. This toolbox highlights thinking routines developed across a number of research projects at the Harvard University Graduate School of Education. A thinking routine is a set of questions or a brief sequence of steps used to scaffold and support a person's thinking.

Here are just a few of my favorite Project Zero thinking routines that Dr. Catlin Tucker, a K-12 edtech leader in California, designed into a collection of Google Slide deck templates. It makes the learning and creative conversations so much more engaging with your colleagues, staff, and students.

LEARNING PHRASES TO ENGAGE IN POSITIVE CONVERSATIONS

Another way to lean in to support conversation is by developing more positive conversations.

It's important to lead with positive, affirmative words. You can make positivity a habit by adding the following to your vocabulary.

- Definitely
- Surely
- Absolutely
- Gladly
- Certainly
- Fantastic
- Great
- Good
- Terrific
- Will
- Assure
- Understand

Another strategy is to start conversations and phrases with positive words, such as the following.

- I completely understand...
- I can definitely help with that...
- I assure you, we most certainly will...
- Fantastic! I'm so glad to be of help...

Use the following key phrases to tap into the part of your colleague, student, or employee that wants to feel more appreciated.

- I see you've been with [Company Name] for X years. That's a long time!

- I appreciate your patience.
- Thank you for remaining so positive.
- Your business means a lot to us.
- I want to thank you for taking the time to speak with me today.

Every leader is also a customer. The following positive statements can connect you to and reassure your employee or customer.

- If I were in your position, I would feel the same way.
- That would frustrate me, too.
- I would be asking the same questions as you are.
- You are totally right.
- I would come to the same conclusion.

In addition to using more positive words, you can also use a more positive, gentle tone of voice. Unfortunately, it can be hard to convey tone if you aren't face to face with a person, such as if you're communicating by text or email. The following phrases can suggest a positive tone and show your colleagues, employees, or customers that their comfort is your priority.

- Personally, I would recommend you to...
- Would you like to try our new XYZ...
- You can consider X.
- You might find X helpful...
- I think you'll find it's much easier if you do X.

Part of leaning in is understanding how to balance two sides of the employee or customer service equation. While people are looking to you for leadership guidance, they also want their opinions to be respected. You can think of this as being assertive with your employee or customer, rather than aggressively steering the conversation, or passively allowing the employee or customer to sit in indecisiveness.

You can ensure that your colleague, student, or employee is onboard with your resolution by asking questions like these.

- What can I do to make your experience better?
- What would be the best-case scenario for you?
- Is there anything else, big or small, that I can help you with today?
- How do you feel about X?
- Are your X needs being met with our product/service?

Use the positive statements below to slow down and restate a person's concern to help ease any anxiety of frustrations. Doing so will pull you back into the moment and help you remember what's unique about your colleague's or student's situation.

- If I am understanding you correctly...
- What you're saying is...
- Did you mean to tell me X?
- Let me know if I'm getting the story right...
- What you're saying is...

Always speak to people the way you would like to be spoken to. To speak more casually, try using combinations of contractions, exclamation mark statements, and shorter, concise sentences. Some examples include the following.

- Thanks for waiting this out.
- I'd love to help you with that.
- Give me just a minute/second while I figure this out for you.
- That's awesome/great!
- I can fix that.

I've given you lots of strategies for more positive conversations. But not all of our conversations can be positive. Did you know you can rephrase almost anything in a more positive light once you know how? When you rephrase an employee's, customer's, or colleague's comment or complaint, you are doing two important things:

- You make her feel heard and understood.
- You clarify what was said so that you don't misunderstand.

> **WOMEN-IN-LEADERSHIP**
>
> For more ways to build your learning confidence with your leadership skills and become more present during critical conversations, check out the women-in-leadership series from the Lean-In organization video portal. I refer to these video clips often to strengthen my leadership skills and to gain new leadership perspectives and points of view.
>
> In the Lean-In organization's video portal, you'll find a growing library of video vignettes, including expert talks, discussion guides, and resources to help you advance your leadership career, identify and interrupt gender bias in the workplace environment, and deepen your critical conversations among your learners to create a stronger, more compassionate workforce.

IMPROVING YOUR ACTIVE LISTENING AND SELF-AWARENESS LEADERSHIP SKILLS

One of the most valuable skills that I have learned in my career is the ability to actively listen to understand another person's point of view. Our ability to listen has a significant influence on our work success, the nature of how our interactions are interpreted by others, and how we respond to others with choice words that reflect we are listening intently. Why do we listen?

- We listen to gather facts.
- We listen to comprehend.
- We listen to have fun.
- We listen to think.

And we listen a lot! Given how much listening we do, you'd think we'd be good at it! In reality, most of us are not. Edgar Dale's Cone of Experience is a model that incorporates several theories related to instructional design and the learning processes. During the 1960s, Edgar Dale theorized that learners retain more information by what they "do" as opposed to what is "heard," "read," or "observed."

Edgar Dale's Cone of Experience outlines that we recall only between 25 and 50 percent of what we hear. To put that into perspective, when you speak to a person for 10 minutes, she probably only retained 5 minutes or less of what you said.

Flip that it around, and you'll realize that you're also not hearing the whole message when you're being given instructions or information. You hope that the 25 to 50 percent of your conversation captures the key pieces, but what if it doesn't?

Clearly, listening is a trait that we all need to improve upon. By becoming a better listener, you can improve your productivity. You can also enhance your ability to influence, persuade, and negotiate. What's more, by becoming a better listener, you'll avoid misunderstandings and conflict. All of these are necessary for workplace success!

A high degree of self-awareness is needed for good communication skills. It has taken me almost 50 years to master this skill. The more you understand your own unique communication style, the better you will be at making positive and lasting impressions with others.

To improve your communication skills, you must communicate to the other person that you are paying attention to what she is saying. To appreciate the significance of this, consider a time when you were talking to someone and you weren't sure she was paying attention. You might have questioned if it was worth your time and effort to talk to her at all.

Signaling to a person that you are listening can be as simple as a nod of the head, a smile, or a simple "uh huh." You are not doing this to convey agreement necessarily—rather, you are signaling that you're paying attention. Using body language and other signals that indicate that you are listening can also assist you in paying attention. Nodding, smiling, and saying "uh huh" can help you to remain focused on the conversation.

The method for improving your listening skills is called "active listening." This is where you make a deliberate attempt to hear the words of another person and also the whole message being conveyed. To do this, you must pay close attention to the other person. You cannot allow yourself to be distracted by what is going on around you, or form counter-arguments while the other person is speaking. You cannot allow yourself to get bored and lose concentration on what the other person is doing.

When you actively listen to what a person is saying, even if you disagree with her point of view, you are showing respect and empathy. You can demonstrate approval, but not necessarily consensus, by nodding or saying things like "I understand" or "I see."

Active listening will give you a sense of the emotions that the speaker is voicing, and keep in mind both the subjective substance and the literal interpretation of the sentences.

Here's a tip I use to be a better active listener: I think of myself like a mirror. When I'm listening to someone, I lean in with interest. At an appropriate time, I restate the speaker's ideas and emotions to her. This shows her that I'm hearing and understanding her clearly. It also confirms the same for me.

I will also interject summary responses to encourage the speaker to continue with her conversation, such as, "So, you do not feel as though you play a strong enough role on the team." Or, "You feel your talents and experiences would be better used in another position." Or, "You feel as though you are undervalued on this project." I present these phrases in a neutral manner so that I do not lead the speaker to my point of view.

An active listener works to keep the speaker from feeling or becoming defensive. There is no need to ask open-ended questions, challenge questions, debate points, or disagree. Priority should now be given to what is said and to how the speaker thinks. To aid in comprehension, repeat the sentence as a question, such as, "Is there anything else you'd rather be doing?"

When you are actively listening, focus on what is not being said rather than on what is being spoken. More often than not, what is held back is as significant as what is spoken. In other words, pay attention to body language. Nonverbal signs like keeping the head down, shifting away from you, or covering the mouth could signal that a person is holding something back or that she feels uncomfortable.

Another part of active listening is to offer your truthful advice when you are asked for it. Be aware of the effect of what you say on others' opinions or ideas, but don't make it difficult for them to think or hinder conversation.

Finally, encourage the speaker to speak openly in order to gain her respect. You help the speaker achieve her desired results, for your group, yourself, and for the business as a whole. If you've already gained her confidence, don't lose it.

When women and girls are empowered to participate fully in society, everyone benefits.
—Melinda Gates

Putting Purpose into Practice

LEAN IN

The following three leadership lean-in strategies will strengthen your cognitive presence and positive genius influence: time, story, and removing "I'm sorry" from our vocabulary.

LEAN IN WITH TIME

Everyone is always strapped for time, so planning for purpose and respecting people's time is so very important. When it is essential to meet, I always include an agenda and stick to it as a lean-in strategy to model the behavior and learning outcomes for all involved, so we can move through the conversations and agenda items efficiently and effectively to respect everyone's time. This shows I respect and value the time commitment that these individuals are providing me as a leader. It is also very important to model your team's agreed-upon norms so all individuals feel safe, their words are honored and respected, and follow-through action steps are put in place to complete the project at hand.

LEAN IN WITH STORY

According to recent Lean-In studies in partnership with Stanford University, women are hardwired to remember stories much more than data, facts, and figures. However, if facts and storylines are combined, listeners can be emotionally impacted. Jennifer Aaker, professor of marketing at the Stanford Graduate School of Business highlights the value of stories and how it persuades people by shaping how they see you is an example of a lean-in strategy and technique that I personally use often to emotional connect to individuals on a personal and professional level. Take a few moments to review this article noted, as you will put into practice the power of stories to persuade others, bring them to action, and make advancements in your leadership career. There is also an opportunity for you to also create your own personal inventory addressing questions to improve your leadership presence with colleagues. For more information on the influence of storytelling be sure to to check out the online resource of Power of Story provided to you from Stanford.

LEAN IN WITHOUT SAYING I'M SORRY

Lastly, yet most importantly, many women leaders get caught up in the "I am sorry trap." We say "I'm sorry" when we have nothing to be sorry about. We have to stop this practice as this is the complete opposite of an effective lean in strategy. We need to devise a go-to lean-in leadership saying to reframe and model our understanding of the situation at hand, while still empathizing with the individuals we are working with in new ways. When you are continually apologizing, you may be appear meek, uncertain, or lack confidence in our leadership presence.

The following five lean-in strategies will help you stop apologizing for everything and to avoid being sorry all the time.

1. Take a breather before apologizing. Until you say sorry, pause and ask yourself:

- Have I really done anything wrong?
- If I didn't do anything wrong, do I really want people to think I feel I did?

If the answer is no, don't apologize.

2. Demonstrate compassion. If you are worried by expressing uncomfortable feelings, bear in mind that there are other ways to express kindness and empathy—rather than apologizing. Instead of apologizing, say something like, "I know that's painful to hear" or, "You can always tell me when you're upset."

3. Recognize your triggers. Write 10 reasons why you want to apologize. For instance, meeting a stranger or asking someone to do something for you. Consider what you might mean instead of each object. Spend a week dwelling on only one, attempting to remove the word "sorry" completely from the context.

4. Don't apologize when asking questions. A time when many women apologize is when posing a question, by saying things like, "I'm sorry to bother you, but can you...." Don't apologize when you inquire. Instead, try things like, "Please say a little bit more about that for me." Or, "Could you please help me understand this better?"

5. Turn apologies into thanks. Often you can rephrase an apology as a statement of thanks. "I'm sorry you had to run that errand," for example, can quickly be transformed into "I'm so glad you gave me this favor!" This is more appealing to the listener, and it also centers the mind on positivity and abundance. This will assist you in attracting even more positivity.

OWN THE ROOM

Here are also some practical lessons that will assist you in becoming a more engaging leader who can captivate any audience at that next staff meeting of educational in-service. One of my favorite resources is called "Own The Room" which is reflective of an effective lean-in leadership teaching practice in the way that people learn today: quickly and by doing. You'll master actionable methods in minutes, not months, thanks to their patented experiential approach. Visit this site for more details, tools, and tips on hosting an Own The Room training at your company. The meeting guide for this video is available here.

Chapter 9

LEADERSHIP CONNECTIONS AND LASTING RELATIONSHIPS

Engage in Learner-Centered Approaches to Influence Others

BUILDING LEADERSHIP CONNECTIONS AND LASTING RELATIONSHIPS

I've been told that my unique personality and enthusiasm to collaborate with others are contagious at times. I believe this is because most of the time I love life, I love my job, I love my family, and I want to portray a positive mindset to focus on the good things in life. You will also come to notice when you spend time with me that I have lots of energy, perhaps a little too much, yet my lens on learning provides a view that may be much different than others. I feel it is very important that everyone has an opportunity to be an active learner and participant in the conversation, so I do more reading of the people in the room techniques to observe the physical body language and interactions from others. I also use my lean-in leadership strategies to be inclusive of a learner-centered and servant leadership mindset. I want to make sure that everyone has a voice to share and the opportunity to be part an active member of the learning process.

As a leader and as a person, I value the connections that I make with other people. One of my favorite ways to connect with someone new is to ask, "How are you currently influencing our world to make it a much better, happier place?" Most people are stunned by this question at first. Then instantly a huge smile lights up their face—and mine.

Most people respond by saying, "You really want me to respond to that open-ended question?"

"Yes, I really want to know more about you and how you are making a difference in our world, personally and professionally," I always answer.

The creative conversation that ensues usually includes them telling me more about themselves, and then they share a little bit more about their jobs and their family. Around this time, I usually notice that a pivotal, influential learning moment has happened in this conversation. I now see that they feel physically and emotionally safe and more comfortable talking with me. That usually is when they share a very special idea or a story they probably haven't shared with others in a long time.

This was the exact reaction that I received from my good friend Maggie from northeast Iowa when I met her for the first time in 2020 with a group of friends from my adolescent years. Maggie is a registered nurse. She changes the lives of people she works with every single day. Maggie's initial reaction to my question was similar to others. But as she opened up to me, with newly gained trust, she expanded upon how she is contributing to a better world. Yet Maggie said she is still trying her best to figure it out everyday. As Maggie talked, I could see her entire body begin to relax, and then she began to tell part of her story with her hands to continue to better express herself. The tone of her voice changed, becoming more excited and enthusiastic. As she spoke, she smiled.

This story illustrates how a leader can connect with and impact another person. An experience like this may bring you joy, hope, and optimism, knowing you have made a positive difference in another person's life even if it's just during one conversation. As you model your cognitive presence and radiate your creative positive genius, you invest in your leadership skills and strengthen your purpose as a lifelong learner and leader.

You make leadership connections with people as you continue to build these new personal or professional relationships with others based on trust and servant leadership strategies. In return, the person has validated her own self-worth, and she has strengthened her own story with confidence. I hope that Maggie gained a new perspective and a creative communication strategy at the same time, to engage and influence others with more creative, collaborative, and deeper conversations as an influential woman leader in the healthcare world to support her leadership and learner-centered approaches to impact others.

When you ask a person a question, connecting with them by showing interest, you build her confidence in her ability to share details about herself. That deepens the conversation—and the connection. Open-ended questions can lay the groundwork to developing closer connections and relationships. They begin conversations where you lean in to engage your friends, family members, or colleagues with learner-centered approaches.

This type of conversation, which focuses on asking open-ended questions and actively listening, models your servant leadership skills. It helps you to better understand and empathize with others. These conversations strategically bring people into the conversation to share their value and their worth. This is when leadership can be transformational. This type of learning is truly better than chocolate!

Meeting the needs of others through lean-in strategies and learner-centered approaches is crucial to build a stronger community of future women leaders—in companies and in educational organizations. Placing people in the center of the learning validates there is a purpose, reason, and humanitarian effort in place to focus on the essential learning needs and outcomes of all involved. It also stresses the importance of how to model effective leadership skills when communicating with your colleagues and what quality communication can look and feel like as a cohesive team approach.

Bringing people together to work collaboratively also validates that each person has a creative gift of knowledge to share. And these new gifts of human perspective, known as diversified knowledge experiences, are the golden tickets of inherent wisdom that will distinguish your business or educational organization from others.

When we are uncomfortable in social settings, some of us seem to overcompensate by talking louder and faster than we normally would. This leads to filling in uncomfortable pauses in the start or the stop of a conversation. At times, we continue to ramble on in streams of consciousness as an effort to hide our nerves, but this is not a good idea either. Epictetus, an ancient Greek philosopher, is credited with writing, "We have two ears and one voice, so we can listen twice as well as we talk." This is one of my favorite quotes, and I use this frequently in my presentations with administrators, teacher leaders, and even students when modeling empathy-based coaching and design thinking scenarios. We all know how irritating it can be to hear someone go on and on about themselves and not take into consideration another person's viewpoint or experience.

For instance, consider sitting next to someone on a plane who goes on and on with his stories and doesn't let you say more than a few words. It can be quite frustrating to be the individual on the receiving end of the conversation. Yet these types of negative experiences are learning opportunities. You learn what not to do. And they reinforce the quality and type of interactions that should be taking place and that we enjoy.

People who are excellent conversationalists are also excellent listeners. Listening closely about what the other person is doing or has to say shows them appreciation, and it also provides you with excellent material for extending the discussion. Where needed, confirm their comments with a nod or a short response. When they come to a longer pause, ask a question depending on what they've taught you or what most intrigued you about their statement. When you listen, look for commonalities between your perspectives or interactions with the other person. These "contact points" will lead to great follow-up questions and the development of a potential partnership. We all like it when we discover something in common with somebody we've just met. That "aha light bulb moment" lights up the room with a happy, fulfilling connection.

One of my relationships perfectly illustrates the idea of building leadership connections and lasting relationships. I had a conversation with a business leader and educator friend Surekha from Dubai. Even though we are thousands of miles apart with an 11-hour timezone difference, we connect on a highly personal and professional level with similar interests. I met Surekha when I gave a keynote address in the Netherlands in Denmark for LEGO Education. We share an interest in STEM and a passion of helping women leaders. We found so much in common at this conference, that we committed to helping each other grow our business leadership strategies and initiatives. We continued to purposefully plan to stay connected and see where our strategic STEM initiatives would take us.

I had planned to support Surekha's STEM initiatives in the spring/summer of 2020, and then the pandemic hit. We did not give up hope. We continued to stay connected by text and video conferencing.

In each conversation that I have with Surekha, our two worlds collide with happy coincidences of learning and leadership experiences that are so similar it brings a smile of gratitude to my face every time we meet. Our most recent conversation landed us in a particularly interesting area, as she reached out to me to support her education design efforts with professional development and to create some engaging and creative educational leadership webinars to support schools in her region. This totally excites me, and I can not wait to support the learning efforts of educational leaders in Dubai.

For these relationships to have real meaning, one needs to make a valiant effort to maintain and invest in people. Relationships must be nurtured. One must demonstrate importance of how and why collaborative leadership and teamwork are essential skills to expand one's presence and influence. Each new people-centered learning experience, we purposefully plan for (or accidentally open up the doorway of opportunity for) lends itself to change the personal and professional lives and mindsets of everyone involved. These encounters will continue to evolve and shape us and the collaborative working teams we lead. We must continue to prioritize our leadership and focus on what is most important to us, and also to the greatest learning impact with the project we are working on or the organization we are leading. We must seek opportunities that have true meaning, and value and identify what we are truly passionate about! And we must say "YES" to the things that truly excite us because as these opportunities will make room for more powerful learning experiences to transform our lives personally and professionally!

I mentioned that a tool that I use to prioritize my to-do list is Pareto's Principle. It's also known as the 80/20 rule. Once I create a to-do list, then I identify my top three priorities. Then I allocate 80 percent of my time to those tasks. The rest of the list gets the remaining 20 percent of my time. This strategy ensures that I'm fully involved and engaged in the top priority tasks. I can devote more creative thinking and process to accomplishing meaningful work.

Here's another way I use the 80/20 rule in my work. I believe that 80 percent of ideas should originate from your team, and 20 percent should originate from you. You will strike this optimal balance if you are delegating, empowering, enabling, coaching, and directing your team properly. When discussing ideas or objectives with team members, many leaders make the mistake of being overly directive. A good example of this is when a manager asks, "What if we do X to fix this problem?" On the surface, this appears to be a question. In truth, the boss only gave a solution concept. A better question to ask is, "What are your ideas for addressing this issue?" With this inquiry, the employee gets the chance to consider options and do most of the brainstorming and talking. Of course, as the leader, you'll be required to and should contribute your thoughts. However, this should be limited to no more than 20 percent of the time.

As a leader, you should spend 80 percent of your time listening to your team and 20 percent talking to them. Your primary role is to guide your team to success with learner-centered approaches.

Unfortunately, many leaders mistake "guide" for "tell them what to do." These "leaders" talk much more than they listen. In actuality, if the leader has effectively staffed their team, established suitable performance objectives, timetables, and offered the necessary amount of coaching, there will be a greater need to listen to the employee's route and development rather than to direct or dictate to the person.

Finally, if you notice that things are not moving at the desired rate or in the desired direction, you may always intervene and remedy the situation. The bottom line is that you, as a leader, should spend significantly more time listening to your staff than directing them.

UNDERSTANDING THE POWER OF NAMES

Through my years in the educational and business leadership space, I've learned that a name means everything! When we use another person's name at the beginning of a conversation, it makes them feel welcome. When you sprinkle their name in throughout the conversation, it makes them feel important and validated. I suggest trying to use a person's name at least three times during your first conversation.

As a bonus, using a person's name will help you to remember it.

We are hard-wired to like knowing our own titles. Dale Carnegie, author of *How to Win Friends and Influence Others* wrote, "Remember that a person's name is to that person the sweetest and most valuable sound in any language."

Using a person's name can be a powerful conversational tool. Hearing others say our name makes us feel respected and valuable. That sense of respect is essential for any good discussion.

"A major reason you don't recall names is you weren't listening," wrote Ron White, winner of the USA Memory Championship in 2009 and 2010 and an international memory speaker. "Someone says their name, and two seconds later you don't know it. This is not a memory problem. It is a focus problem."

Repeating and remembering names is a talent that can be developed. Recognize that it is a talent you wish to improve, and then ask a family member, friend, or coworker to assist you by listening to you speak and offering constructive criticism. Self-motivation, self-discipline, resilience, communication, and social skills will be required. Over time, you'll be able to use a person's name comfortably in conversation, and you might also inspire other people to work on the same skill.

But what if a person has an unfamiliar or difficult-to-say name? Even when I introduce myself to others in conversation, people tend to mix up the vowel enunciation in my name. I intentionally say my name with an emphasis on the long "A" and long "O"—NA - O - Mi. But still I get a lot of NI O MEEs, or NO AM MEEs back. Sometimes I just ignore it, but other times it really bothers me. Sometimes I make a point to pronounce my name with an analogy to Naomi Cambell, the beautiful British model, actress, and businesswoman, and ask the person if they know who she is. Most times they do, and then I mention, "My first name is pronounced just like hers, with the emphasis on the long "A" and long "O" and the "I" on the end sounds like an "E." When I make this point, I know I have their attention. Most of the time, they say my name correctly.

I always tell people how important a name is. When I struggle to pronounce someone's name, I say, "Wow, what a unique name you have" and ask, "Could you say it again to ensure I am pronouncing it correctly?" Then I practice saying their name with them to perfect my pronunciation. This attention to detail and active listening has begun many valuable conversations and leadership connections.

Here are my go-to tips for including and remembering a person's name in your conversations.

- Within the first few minutes of a conversation, say the person's name three times.
- If you have the opportunity, write the name down. Asking for and saving business cards also works nicely.
- Make a visual game out of a name. Imagine that a person has her name tattooed on her forehead or worn on a locket around their neck.
- Sometimes picturing a name is insufficient, and you merely recall a part of the name, for example, the name had four letters and started with a J. Make a sound with the name by pronouncing it out loud.
- Create a funny story based on the name. Things that stand out are remembered, therefore make the name and the face stand out together.
- When you hear a name, inquire about the spelling, such as by asking, "Is Madelyn spelled with an "i" or "y"?
- Compliment it. If you like the name, say so.
- If the name is uncommon, you might inquire about its history or origin.

Stop making excuses about being terrible with names, having a weak memory, or avoiding people because you can't remember their names. Remove the distractions in talks that cause you to forget a person's name. Make a commitment to practicing using and remembering people's names. By remembering a person's name, you demonstrate that you are interested in her, value what she has to say, and appreciate the discussion you are having.

Putting Purpose into Practice

CONVERSATION STARTERS

Conversation starters help to break the ice with a person. They also help you to learn new, interesting things about her. They will foster leadership connections and pave the way for meaningful relationships. Here are my favorite conversation starters. Which will you use to deepen your leadership discussions?

- What favorite family memory has stuck with you into your adult life?
- How do you use the information that you learned in your favorite class in your life today?
- What spectator activities do you most enjoy attending?
- What was the most memorable event that you experienced in college?
- What is the most memorable vacation you've taken?
- What's rocking your world this month?
- What's the craziest thing you've done in your life?
- What's your favorite activity to do locally and why?
- What are three things about you that you think no one here knows?
- What part of your current job is your favorite?
- What's one thing that you love to do that you get to do nearly every day?
- What's your most significant current challenge?
- What would you like to accomplish in your job this year?
- What is your favorite local restaurant?
- What outdoor activities do you most enjoy?
- What is one goal that you plan to accomplish?
- What's your dream vacation?
- What is the best meal that you've ever made?
- If you could only travel to one country, which country would you choose?
- What's your favorite color and why?
- If you had the opportunity to adopt a pet, what kind would you get?
- What are the characteristics of the best visionary leader you ever had?
- What made you smile today?

Finally, remember to smile during the first and subsequent chats because a smile is worth a thousand words. "When your muscles suggest you're pleased, you're more likely to view the world around you in a favorable light," human and artificial cognition expert Fernando Marmolejo-Ramos stated in a news statement. The muscular movements of a grin, according to Marmolejo-Ramos, activate the amygdala—the area of your brain that allows you to sense emotions—by producing neurotransmitters that encourage an emotionally happy state.

"This has intriguing implications for mental health. If we can deceive the brain into viewing stimuli as 'happy,' we may be able to harness this process to improve mental health," Marmolejo-Ramos explained.

Smiling, in other words, tricks the brain into believing you're pleased, which may lead to genuine sensations of happiness and boost your memory by allowing you to remember the person's name, but it doesn't end there. Dr. Murray Grossan, an ENT-otolaryngologist in Los Angeles, claims that stress lowers your immune system while pleasure increases it, citing the science of psychoneuroimmunology (the study of how the brain is related to the immune system).

"What's incredible is that merely the act of laughing can help you acquire immunity," Dr. Grossan explained in an NBC interview. "When you grin, the brain perceives muscle [movement] and interprets it as a source of amusement."

In that sense, the brain is a sucker for a smile. It doesn't matter if you're laughing, genuinely joyful, or simply acting joyful.

Have you ever been approached by someone who appeared to be speaking to you, but instead of looking you in the eyes, glanced down or elsewhere in the room? It's hard to speak with someone who lacks interpersonal connection. A welcoming grin may seem too easy to be real, yet it may be your best friend when seeking to strike up a discussion. A smile is, in fact, the most powerful nonverbal indication we can convey to someone.

I hope you now realize that when we meet and welcome people, our facial expressions tell a mile long story about who we are, so why not put on a happy face and show up every day to reflect and represent your best self? You will be glad you did.

Chapter 10

CELEBRATE THE UNIQUE INDIVIDUAL YOU

Leave a Legacy of Good to Mentor Future Generations of Young Women Leaders

CREATING YOUR LEGACY, STORY, AND POSITIVE INFLUENCE

As a leader, leaving an influential legacy is the most powerful thing you can do in your career and life. It allows you to have influence long after you are no longer in the picture, helping your business and employees to optimize their influence. Legacy can include efforts to secure the company's long-term existence and make it more robust, productive, and valuable than ever before. Or legacy can be building a whole new organization in more extreme instances driven by entrepreneurs. Thinking about your legacy is an excellent strategy to guarantee that you consider your organization's long-term perspective and avoid the temptation of making over-focused, short-term decisions.

So, how can you keep your legacy in mind as you make daily decisions? Fortunately, more than a decade of research on how people make decisions that affect future generations has yielded some tactics to assist you in keeping legacy building in mind and leveraging those ideas to maximize your effect on the world.

First, let's consider the impact of what the preceding generation did for you.

- How did the behaviors of your predecessors influence you?
- What materials did they leave for you and your collaborators?
- How did they alter the organization to make chances of learning opportunities available to you?
- How did they influence the culture of your organization?

While it is not always possible to repay the acts of previous generations because they are no longer a part of the organization, you may pay it forward by acting similarly to the next generation of organizational leaders. When you take a long-term view and see your organization in terms of numerous generations, reciprocity becomes less direct and more broad. According to research, when we are aware that we have benefitted from the legacy of our predecessors, we are more likely to consider the influential legacy we wish to leave for future generations, and we are more likely to make long-term decisions.

Consider the responsibility that comes with your authority.

The majority of research on powerful leadership indicates that the experience of authority tends to increase people's self-awareness and self-interest. This study focuses on the impact of power in short timeframes. Recent research on intergenerational decisions encompassing longer periods, however, suggests that power can cause decision makers to be more concerned with the future interests of others. People feel more of a social responsibility and are more focused on their legacy when intergenerational decisions are mixed with an elevated feeling of power, compared to when their authority is not evident. As a result, they are more charitable to future generations, which naturally aids them in leaving a positive legacy. When it is evident that we can influence the fates of helpless and voiceless individuals, our decisions become more morally charged, and we take the implications of our actions more seriously.

The mark of a strong leader is leaving an impact that continues long after her passing. By using this approach, you may greatly enhance your effect while also supporting the long-term growth of the business. Your legacy is all you have at the end of the day. Let your desire to be remembered by others guide your actions.

Second, create a legacy statement, which is a record of what you want to leave behind for future generations, including your goals, objectives, and desires. It is not a catalog of your achievements, apologies, or failures. It's a record of the things that are most important to your life, the lessons you've learned, and the values you hold dear to your heart both personally and professionally. Here is an example legacy statement.

Your smile is your logo,
Your personality is your V-card,
How you leave others feeling after an experience
with you will become your legacy.

Now you may be wondering where to begin. How do you craft a legacy statement that allows you to be true to yourself while also meeting the demands of your leadership vocation? Let's start with a few quick reflection tips to emphasize from our previous chapters.

In chapter 2, you created a vision board to assist you with creating your visionary roadmap as an innovative method of architecting your personal and professional visual thinking leadership strategies. This process encouraged you to think about your life and learning goals, and how to meet and achieve them. As you may have discovered, your vision board is a guide that continually supports creative structure, consistent action, and a focus on leadership development.

- What two or three phrases best describe your vision board?
- Does it reflect your interest in learning and leadership?
- If so, how does it carry out your legacy message, and if not, what modifications do you need to make and why?

Keep in mind that your legacy statement will serve as a record of what you want to leave to future generations. Legacy statements are nonbinding and are easier to establish than ever before. You could even find examples and help for writing your narrative or legacy statement online.

Sometimes a legacy statement gives the following generation the opportunity to follow a different course, examine fresh ideas, and reflect on the responsibility and leadership of the last generation. A common notion of legacy, defined as a bequest of money or personal property, might impede us from appreciating the importance of our family history. Another definition is anything passed down or obtained from an ancestor or predecessor. Legacies include monetary and property contributions, but they are also the story of our lives, the ideals we attempted to live by, the lessons we learned, and the body we started and hope others will continue.

Here are ideas of what you should include in your legacy statement.

- Identify your most significant beliefs and values.
- Describe your family, job, and community role, all of which is part of your story, your heritage.
- Describe your beliefs and how your life and choices have affected them.
- Relate a memorable experience and how it affected your choices about your life.
- Describe what caused you to laugh, sadden, or perhaps stop reflecting.
- Explain important decisions and hope that the following generation will continue in the spirit of charity.
- Know what others want the future generation to remember.

There is no precise format for a legacy statement. You might consider making it official by signing and dating it, if that would help you stay true to your word and honor your legacy.

Consider sharing your legacy statement it with the next generation, leaving a copy with other crucial documents like your will and estate documents, so your family and friends will remember you for the good and change you made.

Our life narrative is a legacy for most of us. Share your story, as it just might be the most important gift you can provide and leave for the next generation of young women leaders.

DECIDING HOW TO MENTOR YOUNG WOMEN LEADERS

Mentoring is essential for our future of young women leaders, whether the younger generation is being groomed to take over a family business, just graduating into a leadership position at a closely held or public company, or hiring new teachers within a school district to navigate the educational system and modeling effective teaching and learning strategies to impact student learning. The present generation's knowledge and expertise are critical to the younger generation's success and beyond.

Many businesses and educational organizations do not have a plan to prepare these future generations of leaders. According to research, just one out of every eight businesses and school systems has a documented strategy for leadership continuity. Many people believe that drafting a plan is too much, too soon. Scarce training budgets and inadequate resources are additional reasons they ignore such an important component of any organization. When day-to-day operations take precedence over succession planning, months and years pass without addressing this strategic requirement. We see this in education especially and all too often. This will invariably result in a team of leaders and managers who aren't prepared to take command.

What are our options? Mentoring is the solution. It is a low-cost, incredibly successful method of preparing prospective leaders from the start. Mentoring is as easy as giving someone a slight nudge in the correct direction. It's also a simple approach to protect your company's or educational organization's intangible assets—the brains and skills of the essential young people, the talent—who will be the face of your brand in the future. Mentoring promotes the retention of your finest and brightest employees, expands your talent pool, accelerates employee progress, shortens the learning cycle, and fosters loyalty.

The approach to developing a pipeline of future corporate and educational leaders is to assist the younger generation in discovering their calling. The rungs of the career ladder are studded with connections that might propel you to new heights.

The higher I climb the ladder, the more I realize the necessity of giving back and assisting the future generation.
—Vanessa Yanez

Not everyone can just jump into a leadership position. A truly good leader has to be taught how to both lead and follow, to listen and understand, and to speak with compassion and conviction. Yet, what if all women business or educational leaders passed down their knowledge to future generations in their organizations?

The generational divide is frequently the wedge causing bad mentor-mentee interactions. Every generation has its own set of beliefs, goals, and theories about how the world should function. The younger generation, particularly Millennials and Generation Z, views work quite differently than the Baby Boomers or even Generation X. The younger generations are more worried about the balance between work and life than their elders. While the elder generation is used to working long hours, the younger generations are increasingly relying on technology to help with part of the labor, allowing them to pursue hobbies outside of work.

Neither point of view is correct or incorrect. But each age has a tendency to hold on to their beliefs, which can breed animosity and mistrust.

Young employees are often motivated to learn and make a difference. They are technologically aware, extremely flexible, and at ease with change. They are also multiculturally conscious. Companies require these abilities from all of their employees and executives. Younger employees can advise their more senior employers and colleagues in these areas, while established leaders can assist the younger ones in channeling their ideas and excitement in ways that foster innovation.

According to Jeanne Meister, co-author of *The 2020 Workplace*, the mentorship program for Millennials differs from traditional mentorship. Mentoring for this population, for example, should be pushed beyond the face-to-face approach by using social media.

"Millennials respond better to innovative and mature management, suggesting the need for expertise in management while utilizing more up-to-date tactics," Meister wrote.

On-demand, online tutoring appears to be Millennials' best option. It pairs the mentee with a mentor outside the organization by profiling the mentee through psychological tests. The whole mentoring process is then conducted online, and both mentor and mentee remain anonymous. It can be short term or last up to a year.

Take some inspiration from Intel's mentorship program. Anyone, regardless of status, can mentor at this company. One of the company's star mentors is a senior administrative assistant. She's an excellent mentor because she possesses talents that are essential to Intel. She is an expert at getting into the informal communication networks that keep the organization running. Examine your whole organization, from HR to engineering, to identify what common talents might be handed on to others.

As a mentor, following these tips will help you to develop and sustain good mentoring habits and establish and maintain a positive mentoring relationship.

1. Align your objectives. Determine what each party wants from the mentorship and verify that each side's relationship objectives are matched. As the relationship develops, this will assist to avoid misunderstandings and head-butting. While the mentor and mentee may have opposing viewpoints on how to operate the firm, they both want it to flourish. Aligning relationship objectives allows both parties to see the big picture.

2. Make it clear what you expect. As a woman in business and an educational leader, I've often seen animosity grow in mentorship as a result of expectations not being met. Nine times out of 10, the expectations were never communicated effectively, leaving at least one person in the dark about what was going on.

Make it clear if you anticipate your mentee to work a 50-hour week rather than a 40-hour week. Make it explicit if you need something to be completed by a specific day and time. Be as precise as possible. Making your expectations clear can assist you in avoiding increasing animosity and clarifying each person's position in the relationship.

3. Consider mentorship to be a business. Too frequently, I see mentorships deteriorate as a result of being dismissed as inconsequential to leadership development. Mentors and mentees will frequently cancel meetings and place little value on the connection. Mentorships should be approached like a business. Make no excuses. Meetings should not be canceled. Treat your mentee like a customer. Your mentoring meeting may not result in a large sale by the end of the month, but it is critical to the future of your company or educational organization.

4. Use a comprehensive strategy. Mentorships are more than just educating the next generation how to run a business. Use this opportunity to discuss strategy, tactics, and philosophy. If the mentee has a fresh concept for how to enhance the company's workflow of communication, or educational marketing product or streamline program management, discuss it thoroughly supported with a visual, so everyone is on the same page rather than dismissing it.

Examine the mentorship from every viewpoint. How can you assist the mentee both emotionally and strategically? Before handing over the reins, you want your mentee to be skilled, confident, and prepared to take appropriate educational risks.

5. Deepen your relationship with your mentee. In my work as a women's leadership strategist, I frequently see educational mentorships fail because the veteran mentor believes she already knows her new mentee as a second or third year teacher. No matter how close you are to your colleagues of educators or business colleagues, there is a lot they don't tell you. (Trust me.)

MILLION WOMEN MENTORS CORPORATE-COMMUNITY MENTORING PLAYBOOK

This corporate-community mentoring playbook is designed to help you through the phases of developing a successful corporate and educational community mentoring program. In this playbook, you will find recommendations, tools, and frameworks to set you and your corporate mentoring program up for success.

6. Allow mentees to demonstrate their capabilities. The younger generation has fresh perspectives that the older age may not necessarily share. Your mentee may feel that if she can do a task in less time, she would have more spare time. You could complain about her lack of work ethic, but don't. Instead, offer her the opportunity to demonstrate her understanding. Assign your mentee a project and allow her to do it in her own unique style, then observe the outcome. You could be pleasantly surprised!

7. Give it time. It takes time to build effective mentoring strategies. Set realistic, measurable leadership development goals for at least a year. Be flexible as well. As your mentorship connection evolves, adjust the relationship and the goals. Create a safe environment for your mentee to express herself and be candid about her fears. Never dismiss or insult them. A strong mentoring experience is built on effective communication. Maintain open channels of communication and an open mind regarding the next generation. Their growth will eventually determine the fate of your company or educational organization in the future.

The success of every woman should be the inspiration to another.
We should raise each other up. Make sure you're very courageous:
be strong, be extremely kind, and above all be humble.

—Serena Williams

Putting Purpose into Practice

MENTORING TOOLS

By now I know many of you may be looking for more women role modeling and mentoring strategies and activities to better prepare you for the new hat you will wear as an education mentor, role model, or as a career and life coach. For this very reason, I have put this exemplar collection together for you to jump start your STEM and leadership student advocacy with girls and young women, and it is the perfect balance to introduce to your male students as well.

1. Advisor, Teacher, and Role Models
2. Career Girls
3. Challenging Our Gendered Idea Of Mentorship
4. Her-Story Global Collaboration Project
5. Role Models and Mentors
6. Role Model Strategies
7. SciGirls Role Model Profiles
8. STEM Role Models For Mentoring Disabled Students
9. The Roles Woman Can Play as Leadership Mentors
10. Why Girls Need More Mentors in STEM

CELEBRATING STRONG WOMEN LEADERS THROUGH "HER-STORY" GLOBAL COLLABORATION PROJECT

The "Her-Story" Global Collaboration Project is an opportunity for you to guide your students with interviewing a woman leader of influence in your community or a family member, and then create a celebratory multimedia presentation or video documentary biography project about this women leader. The learning outcome of the "Her-Story" final project is to provide powerful learning experiences for ALL K-12 students to empathize with these women leaders of the how/why they have overcome career-work-life challenges, as they persevered to achieve their lifetime dreams and goals in

STEM, CS, and leadership career fields. It is also supported with 10 bonus enrichment activities and 25 bonus choice activities to offer choice and personalize the learning for all of you students to celebrate strong women leaders.

STEM AND COMPUTER SCIENCE HANDS-ON EXPERIENCES AND ACTIVITIES

Sharing is caring, and I would like to provide you with 10 "lean-in and getting started" collection of my top activities to use with students and adult learners. These resources will provide girls and young women of all abilities the necessary hands-on learning experiences to build their learning confidence.

1. Access and play the leadership Mentor Hats card game.
2. Have students design their own Passion to Purpose dream project.
3. Print and play the Women In Science DIY card kit.
4. Engage your entire class in a creative conversation based on this "Motivating Girls to Lean-In" infographic and have students design their own STEM or leadership passion infographic utilizing the free versions of Canva, Ease.ly, Piktocharts, or Google Drawings.
5. Provide students choice of 35 design challenges through Journey to City X Adventures in Engineering for Kids to design their futures.
6. Have students design their own board or card games based on female role models they admire in their communities.
7. Introduce students to vision or dream boards and have them design their own STEM or computer science vision of their future selves demonstrating what change they will contribute to make the world a better place for others.
8. Invite students to participate as a collaborative team in Career Village and ask a woman-in-leadership expert questions about future STEM or computer science career pathways. Or Request a Woman Scientist through Skype a Scientist. Students can ask questions of the scientist to build new knowledge and empathize with her struggles, challenges, and accomplishments.

9. Explore through self-directed choice the SciGirls or Career Girls website of girls, young women, and female role models and mentors to learn from.
10. Write a letter to your future self focused on computer science, STEM, or leadership goals and passions.

BUILD YOUR FUTURE SELF

Challenge your students or even your colleagues to create their future leadership self's through this fun online site of creating your own LEGO mini-figurines or use real LEGO people bricks. Then have your students or colleagues write and create an interesting leadership story of their future selves that is reflective 1, 3, or 5 years out in the future using the *Future.me* website.

Bonus options are to have your students or colleagues create a time capsule letter or presentation of their future selves too from this SlidesMania template.

ENGINEERING A DISH GARDENING

Dish gardens are miniature gardens that combine groups of plants in a decorative container to create fashionable home decor that dresses up a living space with interesting textures, unique shapes, and organic color and can symbolize a memorable time, place and/or person to celebrate their life. According to Bloom IQ, "While the origins of dish gardens are obscure, they are said to have begun centuries ago as a Japanese artistic hobby as well as a model for landscape architects. The leading landscape gardeners of Japan would create miniature models of their work to help customers visualize the end result. Three stones were always placed in these Japanese gardens to symbolize Heaven, Earth, and Mankind. Americans became fascinated by these tiny landscapes when travelers would bring them home from Japan or make them upon their return."

I have introduced this activity in leadership workshops and during my engineering workshops with students, parents, and community members. It lends itself to build a stronger community of leaders while laying the foundational groundwork to build relationship cultures, trust, and represent and celebrate diverse learning styles.

For this activity, have students or your colleagues first sketchnote a drawing of their planned visual dish garden based on the leadership prompt you have provided for them and to represent their legacy statement. Then have your students or colleagues go on a scavenger hunt to seek, find, and collect a variety of outdoor nature elements that can be used with respect to the environment, and use craft supplies that you have at your disposal for your students to create their dish gardens.

Have your students also utilize recycled cans, jars, bins or pots as the base of their dish gardens. Make available some potting soil, succulent plants, gardening tools, and gloves and let the creative engineering and design fun begin.

Make sure to take a few digital photos, too. To contribute, upload to a collaborative shared slide deck to celebrate everyone's final dish gardening projects and their leadership stories.

In Closing

I hope that this book has provided you with further action-oriented leadership concepts to help you lead with empathy, intuition, and collaboration in your business, educational institution, or classroom setting. My mentorship stories of hope, optimism, mindfulness, and resilience are a creative digital toolbox of inspiring strategies supported by researched practices to help you build your leadership visionary roadmap. I'm looking forward to seeing how you utilize the information and ideas from "Putting Your Purpose into Practice" and provided workbook at the end of each chapter to identify and guide your next steps in your women in leadership journey. Most significantly, your new leadership perspective will continue to strengthen your woman's leadership confidence and cognitive presence within your unique sphere of influence.

Every woman has a story to tell to leave her legacy of good in our world. It is these intellectual gifts of wisdom and knowledge, that provide our future generations of young women with hope, optimism, courage, and strength to continue to lead. You see, these young women will continue to build their lifelong learning confidence by the impact of the positive learning experiences from influential women mentors and role models. And all the while, they will continue to rewrite the women in leadership secret code, as they contribute to making their own leadership story and legacy.

Visit this site to access this book's support toolkit of resources and the reflection workbook to support your learning from each chapter.

Resources

CHAPTER 1

The Rancho Los Amigos Levels of Cognitive Functioning Scale is a renowned clinical tool used to rate how people with brain injury are recovering. The ten levels of recovery noted in the scale also help to decide when a patient is ready for rehabilitation. As patients "wake up" after a head injury, they go through different levels of recovery on the Rancho Scale. Each level describes a general pattern of recovery, with a focus on cognition and behavior. The Rancho Skills Matrix brain injury neuroscience study can be found at https://www.matrixneurological.org/information/fact-sheets/brain-injury-stage-recovery-ranchos-scale

CHAPTER 2

"Can a Vision Board Really Affect Your Future?" How Stuff Works, https://science.howstuffworks.com/life/inside-the-mind/human-brain/vision-board.htm

"Few Women Run the Nation's School Districts. Why?" Ed Week, https://www.edweek.org/leadership/few-women-run-the-nations-school-districts-why/2016/11

"Gender-Based Cerebral Perfusion Differences in 46,034 Functional Neuroimaging Scans," by Daniel G. Amen et al, Journal of Alzheimer's Disease, https://content.iospress.com/articles/journal-of-alzheimers-disease/jad170432

"How to Improve Teamwork in the Workplace," Gallup, https://www.gallup.com/cliftonstrengths/en/278225/how-to-improve-teamwork.aspx

"What Is the Hippocampus?" Medical News Today, https://www.medicalnewstoday.com/articles/313295

"What Makes a Team Smarter? More Women," Harvard Business Review, https://hbr.org/2011/06/defend-your-research-what-makes-a-team-smarter-more-women

"Women in the Workplace 2020," https://www.mckinsey.com/featured-insights/diversity-and-inclusion/women-in-the-workplace

CHAPTER 3

"Importance of Awareness, Support, and Inner Strength to Balance Everyday Life," BMC Women's Health, https://www.ncbi.nlm.nih.gov/pmc/articles/PMC6327387

"Innovator's Compass," https://innovatorscompass.org

"Meaning and Purpose at Work," Better Up, https://f.hubspotusercontent40.net/hubfs/9253440/Asset%20PDFs/Promotions_Assets_Whitepapers/BetterUp-Meaning&Purpose.pdf

"Servant Leadership" Mind Tools, https://www.mindtools.com/pages/article/servant-leadership.htm

"Tarr's Toolbox," Class Tools, www.classtools.net/blog

"Umbrella Sky Project," https://www.impactplan.pt/en/umbrella-sky-project-toulouse16

"Well-Being in Life and Well-Being at Work: Which Comes First? Evidence From a Longitudinal Study," Front Public Health, https://www.ncbi.nlm.nih.gov/pmc/articles/PMC7160299

CHAPTER 4

Scott Frothingham, "How Long Does It Take for a New Behavior to Become Automatic?" Healthline, October 24, 2019,https://www.healthline.com/health/how-long-does-it-take-to-form-a-habit

Anne Trafton, "Electrical Properties of Dendrites Help Explain Our Brain's Unique Computing Power," MIT News, October 18, 2018, https://news.mit.edu/2018/dendrites-explain-brains-computer-power-1018

"5 Books Worth a Read for Women in Leadership," by Nicole Carpenter, Women's Leadership Institute, February 22, 2018, https://wliut.com/book-list-women-in-leadership

"5 Health Benefits of Walking: 20 Minutes a Day Makes a Difference," ThinkHealth, April 17, 2021, https://thinkhealth.priorityhealth.com/health-benefits-of-walking-20 minutes-a-day-makes-a-difference

"6 Key Servant Leadership Attributes," by Dirk van Dierendonck, IEDP, September 26, 2011, https://www.iedp.com/articles/six-key-servant-leader-attributes

"80/20 Rule for Educators," by Danielle Nuhfer, Teaching Well, October 16, 2016, https://teachingwell.life/the-8020-rule-for-educators

"83 Benefits of Journaling for Depression, Anxiety, and Stress," by Courtney E. Ackerman, Positive Psychology, May 19, 2021, https://positivepsychology.com/benefits-of-journaling

"Benefits of Journaling," Positive Psychology, https://positivepsychology.com/benefits-of-journaling

"Electrical Properties of Dendrites Help Explain Our Brain's Unique Computing Power," by Anne Trafton, MIT News, October 18, 2018, https://news.mit.edu/2018/dendrites-explain-brains-computer-power-1018

"How Long Does It Take for a New Behavior to Become Automatic?" by Scott Frothingham, Healthline, October 24, 2019, https://www.healthline.com/health/how-long-does-it-take-to-form-a-habit

"Unrealized Potential of Learning through Play at School," LEGO Education, https://education.lego.com/v3/assets/blt293eea581807678a/blt372bbdd282c6d7e6/5f83ff5a0fa6ca0be8c86d09/le%20learning%20through%20 play%20whitepaper%20digital%20pdf

"What Is Servant Leadership?" Robert K. Greenleaf Center for Servant Leadership, https://www.greenleaf.org/what-is-service-leadership

To learn more about essential oils or purchase some for your own use, contact Jamie Peterson, a wellness advocate and doTERRA essential oils consultant, at beepurebyjamie@gmail.com or on her Essential Oil Facebook group, https://www.facebook.com/beepurebyjamie

"5 Health Benefits of Walking: 20 Minutes a Day Makes a Difference," ThinkHealth, April 17, 2021, https://thinkhealth.priorityhealth.com/ health-benefits-of-walking-20 minutes-a-day-makes-a-difference

Courtney E. Ackerman, "83 Benefits of Journaling for Depression, Anxiety, and Stress," Positive Psychology, May 19, 2021, https://positivepsychology. com/benefits-of-journaling

To learn more about essential oils or purchase some for your own use, I recommend contacting Jamie Peterson, a wellness advocate and doTERRA essential oils consultant, at beepurebyjamie@gmail.com or on her Essential Oil Facebook group, https://www.facebook.com/beepurebyjamie, and through her master classes. Tell her Naomi Harm sent you as an introduction to start the learning and healing conversation with natural essential oils.

Nicole Carpenter, "5 Books Worth a Read for Women in Leadership," Women's Leadership Institute, February 22, 2018, https://wliut.com/book-list-women-in-leadership

"What Is Servant Leadership?" Robert K. Greenleaf Center for Servant Leadership, https://www.greenleaf.org/what-is-service-leadership

Dirk van Dierendonck, "6 Key Servant Leadership Attributes," IEDP, September 26, 2011, https://www.iedp.com/articles/six-key-servant-leader-attributes

Danielle Nuhfer, "The 80/20 Rule for Educators," Teaching Well, October 16, 2016, https://teachingwell.life/the-8020-rule-for-educators

CHAPTER 5

"5 Reasons Why Feedback May Be the Most Important Skill," Cambridge University Press, https://www.cambridge.org/elt/blog/2014/03/17/five-reasons-feedback-may-important-skill

"10 Tips for Teachers Using the Station Rotation Model," Catlin Tucker, https://catlintucker.com/2018/09/10-tips-station-rotation-model

"Building Kids Resilience Through Play Is More Crucial Than Ever," Scientific American, https://blogs.scientificamerican.com/observations/building-kids-resilience-through-play-is-more-crucial-than-ever

"Compassionate Leadership," Lean In, https://leanin.org/meeting-guides/compassionate-leadership

"Differentiated Instruction," Edutopia, https://www.edutopia.org/topic/differentiated-instruction

"Filmstrips and Education," Retro Edtech, https://www.retroedtech.com/2012/09/filmstrips-and-education_2.html

"Instructional Strategies to Build Student Capacity," ASCD, https://www.ascd.org/el/articles/instructional-strategies-to-build-student-capacity

"Learner-Centered Innovation," Kate L. Marin, https://katielmartin.com/2018/02/06/learner-centered-innovation

"Making a Difference for Girls in STEM," Microsoft, https://www.microsoft.com/en-us/corporate-responsibility/skills-employability/girls-stem-computer-science

"Personalized Learning," K-12 Blueprint, https://www.k12blueprint.com/toolkits/personalized-learning

"Role Models and Mentoring," NGC Project, https://ngcproject.org/role-models-and-mentoring

"Why Do Girls Lose Interest in STEM?" Microsoft, https://news.microsoft.com/features/why-do-girls-lose-interest-in-stem-new-research-has-some-answers-and-what-we-can-do-about-it

"Women in Leadership Cornell Certificate Program," Cornell University, https://ecornell.cornell.edu/certificates/leadership-and-strategic-management/women-in-leadership

"Women in the Workplace 2020," https://ngcproject.org/role-models-and-mentoring

CHAPTER 6

"7 38 55 rule of Communication," Tools Hero, https://www.toolshero.com/communication-skills/7-38-55-rule

"Case for Emotional Intelligence," Six Seconds, https://www.6seconds.org/case

"Create Unforgettable Experiences," Goose Chase, https://www.goosechase.com

"Creative Type Test," https://mycreativetype.com

"EQ in the Navy and Marine Corps," 6 Seconds, https://www.6seconds.org/2011/06/23/case-navy-change

"Intelligence," American Psychological Association, https://www.apa.org/topics/intelligence

"Intelligence," Psychology Today, https://www.psychologytoday.com/us/basics/intelligence

"Importance of Empathy in the Workplace" Center for Creative Leadership, https://www.ccl.org/articles/leading-effectively-articles/empathy-in-the-workplace-a-tool-for-effective-leadership

"Mayer and Salovey Model of Emotional Intelligence," The Institute, http://www.theeiinstitute.com/what-is-emotional-intelligence/4-mayer-and-salovey-model-of-emotional-intelligence.html

"Six Thinking Hats Provide Strong Stimulus for Ideation," MG Rush, https://mgrush.com/blog/debono-six-thinking-hats

"Why is emotional intelligence important for children, families, and educators?" 6 Seconds, https://www.6seconds.org/education/school-case-ebook

CHAPTER 7

"Establishing and Maintaining Boundaries in Teacher-Student Relationships," New Directions for Youth Development, https://ericed.gov/?id=EJ1003222

"How to Set Healthy Boundaries," Positive Psychology, https://positivepsychology.com/great-self-care-setting-healthy-boundaries

CHAPTER 8

"Dale's Cone of Experience," https://www.queensu.ca/teachingandlearning/modules/active/documents/Dales_Cone_of_Experience_summary.pdf

"Develop Leadership Skills," Lean In, https://leanin.org/education#leadership

"Developing Self-Awareness," Mind Tools, https://www.mindtools.com/pages/article/developing-self-awareness.htm

"Harnessing the Power of Stories," https://cdn-media.leanin.org/wp-content/uploads/2013/03/HarnessingStories3.15.pdf

"How to Have Difficult Conversations and Stay True to Yourself," Lean In, https://leanin.org/education/managing-difficult-conversations#!

"Own the Room," https://owntheroom.com/training-programs

"Power of Story," Stanford Graduate School of Business, https://powerofstory.stanford.edu

"Project Zero's Thinking Routines Toolbox," Project Zero, http://www.pz.harvard.edu/thinking-routines

"Support Online Learning with Powerful Thinking Routines," Catlin Tucker, https://catlintucker.com/2020/09/online-learning-thinking-routines

"Thinking Routines," Project Zero, http://www.pz.harvard.edu/projects/visible-thinking

CHAPTER 9

"Transform Your Brain," Ron White, www.ronwhitetraining.com

CHAPTER 10

"Journey to City X," Brett Schilke, https://www.brettschilke.com/book

"Learning Continuity," Michigan Virtual, https://michiganvirtual.org/research/publications/learning-continuity-planning-considerations-for-school-leaders

"Motivating Girls To "Lean In," Piktochart, https://create.piktochart.com/output/35716537-naomiharmmotivatinggirlsstem

“Sci Girls,” PBS Kids, https://pbskids.org/scigirls/profiles

“Skype a Scientist,” https://www.skypeascientist.com

“To Pursue Passion Driven Careers in STEM Purpose through Passion,” Convergence Design Lab, https://convergencedesignlab.org/web-resources/passion-to-purpose

“Women in Science DIY Kit,” https://www.luanagames.com/en.pdf

“Write a Letter to the Future,” Future Me, https://www.futureme.org

Acknowledgments

People wanting to grow and invest in other people's creative leadership talents make our world a better place every day. Additionally, individuals who spend their life sharing their creative talents with our future leaders by coaching and mentoring make it even better. Thanks to everyone who seeks to develop themselves and invest in other people's proven leadership strategies to grow and nurture the intellect of the greater community. This shared collaborative leadership vision is known as the "Circle of Life" from *The Lion King*.

A huge gratitude of thanks to my dedicated husband, Jeff Harm, who still to this day provides amazing quality and compassionate care for our son, so Jacob can experience his best life.

I also want to acknowledge my son Jacob Harm, who has provided me the opportunity as mother and teacher to support him on his continued road to recovery from his TBI and physical disabilities from his Army accident. He has taught me how to be a better listener, teacher, and caregiver—yet, most importantly, how to handle change and the importance of resilience and optimism when faced with the adversity of a serious life-changing event. He makes me a better person every single day!

Thanks to Renee and Rick Matt, my sister and brother-in-law, and their entire family for supporting our family during life's most difficult challenge when our son incurred his Army accident and recovery.

Thank you to those individuals I have had the opportunity to lead, be led by or be inspired by observing their leadership from a distance. They have encouraged me to write and share my effective leadership approaches and lean-in strategies to build a stronger community and culture of future leaders.

This book would not exist if it weren't for the teaching and learning experiences and support of my women in leadership team through my Innovative Educator Consulting Corporation. Each of you has given me the opportunity to lead a fantastic group of courageous, talented and creative educational leaders, and a leader among excellent women leaders is a great place to be.

Your dedicated support throughout the years is especially worthy of a huge gratitude mention: Deb Norton, Velvet Holmes, Valerie Verhunce, Stacci Barganz, Angie Kalthoff, Maria Garbisch, Mariah Richards, Kristin Sandgren, Kathleen Stephany, Helen Xiong, Monica Isabel Martinez, Rebecca Gustafson, Sonja Twedt, and Vanessa Jones. My Innovative Educator Consulting Corporation master educators and EdTech influencers, thank you for being part of my company's incredible women-in-leadership team! Thanks also to my very first creative tech expert hires in 2009, Dan and Sally.

Your collaborative and creative team efforts on the professional development content you have designed and delivered has prepared thousands of educators to transform their teaching and learning leadership practices with students, teachers, and administrators. Yes, each of you has definitely moved the technology literacy needle in the schools we have worked with nationwide, and each of you has contributed to the global success of my Innovative Educator Consulting Corporation.

Special thanks to Emily Balfanz, owner of Emily Jean Photography emilyjeanphoto.com and photographer of my professional branding photos.

I also want to convey my deepest gratitude of appreciation to Jennifer Bright, CEO of Bright Communications and her entire women in leadership publishing creative team. I was so grateful for the high level of communication and collaboration from bi-monthly video meetups with Jennifer to provide feedback on each chapter of my book, to copyediting and wordsmithing with Amy and Jennifer, to Kristen, the graphic artist designer, who really listened to the visual and emotional tone of the book cover I wanted to portray and the custom design and layout of each chapter. By Jennifer's leadership and guidance, she provided me with an amazing writing and publishing experience that was truly joyful. It also encouraged me to expand my writing and research skills to craft the perfect women in leadership storyline that was reflective of my ideas, my words, and my women in leadership legacy message.

I also wish to thank:

• Leota Compton, Sonja Young, Nan Kember, and Kristin Gonia-Larkin: my Bangor Elementary WI first women-in-leadership educator mentors

- Myrna Daugherty, Jodi Hoscheit, Jerry Freimark, Carol Popelka, and Jan Wee: my West Salem, WI administrative leadership and technology mentors who have provided the opportunity to earn my "wisdom glitters" with honor and dignity
- Russel Tarr, my creative and inspiring educator friend from Toulouse, France
- Jack and Iola Hemesath, my father and grandmother from northeast Iowa who are no longer with us, yet their compassionate learning experiences have provided me my unique individual roadmap of life lessons and positive influences
- Ela Ben-Ur, my inspiring educator friend and the creator of the Innovator's Compass
- Mae Becker, my inspirational and compassionate 3rd/4th grade classroom teacher from Northeast Iowa at St. Francis de Sales Schools
- Kathleen Kersznowski, an EdTech leader in New Jersey and a very good educator friend
- Dr. Catlin Tucker, a K-12 EdTech leader in California who is making phenomenal strides in education
- Maggie Weidemann, my good friend from Northeast Iowa who is a courageous, compassionate registered nurse
- Jamie Peterson, my wellness advocate at doTERRA Essential Oils
- Surekha Kembhavi, my international woman-in-leadership friend and EdTech influencer from Dubai, United Arab Emirates

In closing, I also want to celebrate and acknowledge every woman mentioned from the story line of this book. Each of our intentional and accident interactions has contributed to my personal and professional leadership growth. By each of you modeling and giving your time, expertise, and active listening mentor moments, it has provided me the greatest gift of transforming my women in leadership career trajectory. Thanks to each of you for supporting my visionary roadmap to lead with empathy, collaboration, and intuition as a confident woman leader in the global EdTech space!

About the Author

Naomi Harm has more than 25 years of experience as an educator, women-in-leadership strategist and mentor, and EdTech influencer. Her main leadership and speaking engagements focus on how to create dynamic and inclusive learning experiences to support the diverse needs of today's Generation Z and Gen Alpha students with K-12 educational leaders, university professors, and managers and directors in business leadership roles. She has been involved in leading school district reform initiatives, redesigning classroom spaces and learning experiences with the brain in mind, professional development, and curriculum alignment with ISTE standards, administrative leadership symposiums and roundtables, and developing and implementing STEM mentoring and role modeling leadership programs for girls, young women, and aspiring women leaders globally.

CPSIA information can be obtained
at www.ICGtesting.com
Printed in the USA
LVHW071755290422
717570LV00009B/767

9 781952 481611